CHINA'S
FIRST EMPEROR
—— AND THE ——
TERRACOTTA
WARRIORS

JAMES CS LIN AND XIUZHEN LI

EDITED BY
KAREN MILLER

First published in 2018 by
National Museums Liverpool
127 Dale Street
Liverpool
L2 2JH

On the occasion of the World Museum exhibition *China's First Emperor and the Terracotta Warriors*. This exhibition was organised by National Museums Liverpool, UK and the Shaanxi Provincial Cultural Relics Bureau and Shaanxi Cultural Heritage Promotion Centre, People's Republic of China.

Text copyright:

National Museums Liverpool
World Museum Liverpool
William Brown Street
Liverpool
L3 8EN
UK

Shaanxi Cultural Heritage
Promotion Centre
91 Xiao Zhai East Road
Xi'an, Shaanxi Province
People's Republic of China

Images copyright: see page 148

ISBN 978-1-902700-59-5

Designed by Adrian Hunt
Printed by Generation Press, UK

Front cover Charioteer
Qin Dynasty (221-206 BC)
Terracotta, 191 cm
Emperor Qin Shihuang's Mausoleum Site Museum

Back cover and pp. 2-3 Rows of warriors
Inside front cover Terracotta Warriors and horses
Inside back cover Warriors as found in the pit

Frontispiece Armoured infantry
Qin Dynasty (221-206 BC)
Terracotta, 179 cm
Emperor Qin Shihuang's Mausoleum Site Museum

CONTENTS

FOREWORD

The Qin Dynasty represents the most important milestone in Chinese history. In 221 BC, the first unified, feudal, multi-ethnic, and centralised Qin Empire was established, which marked the beginning of several thousand years of imperial rule in China, and had profound implications for the development of Chinese civilisation. Fortunately in 1974, a farmer digging a well in Lintong County, east of Xi'an in Shaanxi Province, unexpectedly stumbled upon a terracotta warrior pit adjoining the Mausoleum of Qin Shihuang. Subsequent archaeological surveys and excavations confirmed the stunning scale of the site, which became one of the most important Chinese archaeological finds of the 20th century. In 1987, the Mausoleum Complex of Qin Shihuang and three pits of the Terracotta Army were listed as a UNESCO Would Heritage site.

This exhibition, *China's First Emperor and the Terracotta Warriors*, features one hundred and twenty five impressive sets of cultural artefacts carefully selected from thirteen archaeological institutes and museums in Shaanxi Province, including those from Emperor Qin Shihuang's Mausoleum Site Museum, Shaanxi History Museum, and Han Yangling Museum. These exhibits include not only the life-sized terracotta figures in various postures with different facial expressions, but also the exquisite gold, silver, bronze, ceramic, and jade objects. These objects show clearly the path by which the Qin grew from a small fiefdom into a vast empire, and present the latest research results on the accomplishments of the Qin in political, economic, military, and cultural areas.

With great support from the Chinese and British governments, in 2015, the Shaanxi Province Cultural Relics Bureau and National Museums Liverpool started to plan an exhibition about the Qin culture by focusing on the terracotta warriors in Britain. The partners aimed to produce a creative design for its content and style and sought to provide the general public in Britain with updated research within the exhibition: *China's First Emperor and the Terracotta Warriors*.

Cultural artefacts are a crystallisation of human wisdom, products of historical civilisation, and also serve as a bridge of communication. Following three years of careful planning, this exhibition will provide an excellent opportunity for the British public to gain a better understanding of an eastern country more than 2,000 years ago. It will also serve to enhance cultural exchange, mutual understanding and friendship between China and Britain.

Mr Zhao Rong
Director General, Shaanxi Provincial Cultural Relics Bureau

致 辞

秦代是中国历史朝代中最重要的里程碑。公元前221年，中国历史上第一个统一的、多民族、封建制、中央集权的大秦帝国的建立，无疑是中国数千年帝制的肇始，对中华民族文明的推展，带来深远的影响。1974年陕西省西安以东的临潼，在农民掘井的过程中，意外发现了秦始皇陵陪葬的兵马俑坑，出土的文物规模之庞大，举世震惊，成为全球瞩目的焦点，并成为中国二十世纪最重要的考古发现之一，1987年秦兵马俑坑与秦始皇帝陵一起已被联合国教科文组织列入世界文化遗产名录，被誉为"世界第八大奇迹"。

本次《秦始皇和兵马俑》展览，精选了陕西省的包括秦始皇博物馆、陕西历史博物馆、汉阳陵博物院等在内的13家文博单位，共125件组文物精品，这其中不仅包括众为期待的10件神态各异、与真人比例一样大小的兵马俑，还包括金银器、青铜器、陶器、玉器等文物精品，全面展现秦人从蕞尔小国发展壮大直至走向天下一统波澜壮阔的历史轨迹，以及关于秦文化在政治、经济、军事、文化等方面的最新研究成果。

在中英两国政府大力支持与推动下，陕西省文物局与利物浦国家博物馆，于2015年起就开始积极筹划在英国举办中国以兵马俑为主题的秦文化展览，并力求通过展览内容和展览形式上的创新与突破，给广大英国民众呈现出一个结合了最新研究成果和《秦始皇和兵马俑》展览。

文物是人类智慧的结晶，是历史文明的载体，也是构筑和沟通人们心灵的桥梁。经过三年的精心筹划与认真准备，此次展览一定会为英国广大观众提供一个了解两千多年前来自遥远的东方国度秦人真实生活和宏伟帝国面貌的极好机会，对于促进中英文化交流、增进两国民众之间的理解和友谊，也必将产生十分积极的作用。

赵荣
陕西省文物局局长

FOREWORD

This exhibition is a tremendous coup, not just for Liverpool, but for the whole of the UK. As home to one of the oldest Chinese communities in Europe, Liverpool is absolutely the right place for this exhibition, and we are hugely excited to be working with our museum colleagues in China to bring a collection of Warriors, and many other significant historical discoveries to the UK.

We would particularly like to thank our colleagues from Shaanxi Provincial Cultural Relics Bureau, Shaanxi History Museum, Shaanxi Cultural Heritage Promotion Center, Emperor Qin Shihuang's Terracotta Army Museum, Shaanxi Provincial Institute of Archaeology, Han Yangling Museum, Xianyang Museum, Xianyang Cultural Heritage Conservation Center, Xing Ping Museum, Chang Wu County Museum, Mao Ling Museum, Baoji Archeological Working Team, Long Xian County Museum and Qi Shan County Museum. We would also like to express our sincere thanks to Mr Zhao Ou, our Exhibition Coordinator in China, who has assisted us with the exhibition.

We would like to thank Dr James CS Lin and Dr Xiuzhen Li for writing the text for this exhibition catalogue. Many staff at National Museums Liverpool have worked tirelessly to make this exhibition a success, but I must mention in particular Sharon Granville, who has been a tower of strength without whom we could never have achieved so much.

The Terracotta Warriors have found incredible fame around the world since they were discovered by chance in 1974, and this is a once in a lifetime opportunity to see them in Liverpool. We thank our partners in this endeavour, including the Department for Digital, Culture, Media and Sport. I urge everyone to attend this 'must see' show, the highlight of Liverpool's 10th anniversary celebrations as European Capital of Culture in 2018.

David Fleming
Director, National Museums Liverpool

序言

此次展览的举办对利物浦，乃至整个英国，都是一件大事。作为拥有欧洲最古老华人社区的利物浦，在此举办兵马俑展览绝对是最佳选择之一。我们万分激动能与中方博物馆合作，共同努力将兵马俑及其他考古中的重要发现带到英国。

在此，我们由衷感谢陕西省文物局、陕西历史博物馆、陕西省文物交流中心、秦始皇帝陵博物馆、陕西省考古研究院、汉景帝阳陵博物馆、咸阳博物馆、咸阳市文物保护中心、兴平市博物馆、长武县博物馆、茂陵博物馆、宝鸡市考古工作队、陇县博物馆和岐山县博物馆的全体工作人员。我们同样要感谢赵欧先生对本次展览的推动。

同时，万分感谢林政昇博士和李秀珍博士为我馆编写展览图录。还要感谢我馆参与此次活动的同事，为了展览的成功举办凤夜匪懈。特别感谢莎伦·格兰维尔，没有她的鼎力支持，我们不会取得如此巨大的成就。

1974 年，一个偶然发现使秦始皇兵马俑成为举世闻名的考古发现之一，这也许是此生唯一一次在利物浦目睹兵马俑风采的机会。再次感谢所有合作伙伴，以及数字、文化、媒体和体育部门的配合。秦始皇和兵马俑展览是庆祝利物浦荣获"欧洲文化之都"称号十周年的纪念活动之一，我诚挚地邀请每一位观众莅临参观。

戴维·弗莱明
利物浦国家博物馆馆长

INTRODUCTION

JAMES CS LIN

The chance discovery in 1974 of the world-famous Terracotta Warriors was one of the most extraordinary finds ever made, and truly took historians by surprise. Brightly painted and buried in battle formation, the life-size army would protect for eternity one of the most influential leaders of all time - China's First Emperor, Qin Shi Huang. Meticulous excavations over the last 40 years have revealed almost 2,000 sculptures, however it is estimated that there are a staggering 8,000 warriors and horses in total. Site surveys have also revealed that the Terracotta Army is only one part of the Emperor's grand preparations for the afterlife, and that nearly 600 burial pits surround his mausoleum, making it the largest and most opulent tomb complex ever constructed.

Qin Shi Huang was the First Emperor of China, unifying the country in 221 BC. This publication, and the exhibition it accompanies, consider the ruler, his achievements and his legacy. How did he establish the Qin Dynasty and become China's First Emperor? What drove him to make such extensive preparations for his burial?

It is useful for readers to understand the Emperor's monumental mausoleum in the context of Chinese burial practice, so chapter one looks back 4,500 years to the Neolithic period, a time before written records. The archaeology from this period reveals a diversity of cultures, and the emergence of cultural themes that recur throughout this publication: belief in an afterlife, ancestor worship, and the importance of protecting both the body and spirit of the deceased, often through the use of jade.

Fig 2 Columns of warriors

We look at the burials of cultures including the Liangzhu (c 2500 BC) and Hongshan (c 3500-2500 BC), and discuss the Bronze Age of the Shang Dynasty (c 1600-1050 BC) and the Western Zhou (c 1050-771 BC).

To understand the success of Qin Shi Huang, chapter two traces his family origins back to the Spring and Autumn Period (770-475 BC), a time before the unification of China when rival states fought for supremacy. We consider the Zhou royal family's move eastwards, and how China spilt into more than one hundred independent states after the family's decline. We discuss the Qin's subsequent emergence as a powerful dynastic force capable of unifying China in 221 BC.

Chapter three focuses on the Qin period, the First Emperor himself and his ill-fated search for immortality. We examine the Emperor's enormous construction projects including the defensive walls, numerous palaces and countrywide transport systems. His administrative reforms, including the standardisation of systems of weight, currency and writing, may seem minor achievements in comparison but were instrumental in creating a unified China.

The Terracotta Warriors are introduced in chapter four. We examine their design and production, but also take a wider perspective by looking at the tomb complex itself. How does the First Emperor's tomb fit into the natural landscape? What were the roles of geomancy and *fengshui*? What does the complex tell us about the Qin Dynasty? How did the First Emperor intend to rule in the other world?

The achievements and advances of the short-lived Qin Empire were adopted by the Han Dynasty (206 BC-AD 220), the focus of chapter five. We look at Han royal tombs and their contents, discussing how the Han prepared for the afterlife, their pursuit of immortality, and why jade played a major part in Han burials. Like the First Emperor of China, emperors of the Han Dynasty and its successors were buried with terracotta figures, intended to protect and serve them in the afterlife. The final chapter will also examine Han contact with the outside world following the establishment of the Silk Route, and why the Han period is considered the Golden Age of Chinese history.

Each stage of our story is illustrated by beautiful and important objects. A wide selection of pieces in a variety of materials, many from Shaanxi Province, have been selected to illustrate this catalogue.

This book shows that although the First Emperor of China did not find the elixir of immortality he sought, and died at just 49 years of age, in some ways he did achieve his objective. His far-reaching construction projects, both above and below ground, may never be surpassed by any Chinese ruler. His influence on the Han and subsequent Chinese society is still felt, and archaeologists and tourists alike still flock to his mausoleum. No doubt future surveys of the burial site will reveal surprising new discoveries and constantly remind us of the first, and also the most ambitious, emperor in Chinese history.

Fig 3 Warriors that retain their original colouration

CHAPTER 1

ANCIENT CHINA

James CS Lin

Modern day China is a vast country: the third largest in the world, 9.6 million km² and bordered by 14 other states. It is a geographically varied landscape, with plateaus, plains, lakes, deserts and mountains, all of which have contributed to it being a culturally diverse country. Even today there are many different regions - homes to people who still have their own distinctive languages, customs and religions.

Before the unification of China under the First Emperor in 221 BC, many states had their own systems of government, writing, currency, units of measurement and even chariot designs, as well as religious beliefs, languages and cultures. This diversity is evident in the archaeology that has been uncovered. The graves of the wealthiest people and the objects

(previous page)
Detail of Fig 14, ritual wine container with Zhong Jiang 中姜 inscription

Fig 4 Map of modern China

Fig 5 China has a
diverse landscape

they contain are especially important as they are often the only evidence
that has survived of this ancient civilisation.

China's recorded history dates back to the Shang Dynasty (c 1600-1046
BC), and is seen in the form of oracle bones; the burnt, cracked and then
engraved animal bones and shells used in divination. The first systematic
historical text, the *Shiji* (Records of the Grand Historian), written by Sima
Qian (c 145-86 BC) covers the period from the legendary Yellow Emperor
(dates unknown) to the historian's own lifetime. However, *Shiji* and
other contemporary texts usually make little or no reference to areas
outside the Yellow River region which were considered to be barbarian.
Archaeological excavations can help us to understand what happened in
this vast, divided region long before it was unified and later named China.

NEOLITHIC CHINA
(C 6000-1700 BC)

In the absence of a written history from this period archaeological discoveries are the sole source of evidence about Neolithic people and their cultures. Excavations have revealed numerous tombs and sites dating from the Neolithic Period onwards all over modern China, many of which belonged to higher status individuals. Most of the objects found are tools, weapons and ornaments; valuable objects that people believed would be required in the afterlife. Differences in the size and number of objects found in these burials indicate a highly complicated social structure in China at that time.

Jade was, and still is, regarded as a precious stone with magical power by Chinese people. Its role in Chinese culture has changed with China's imperial landscape, but it is still valued for its beauty, its symbolism and the power it is believed to possess. It was a very important material in Neolithic China, and has been found in almost every excavated burial.

Fig 6 Archaeological sites of the Neolithic Period

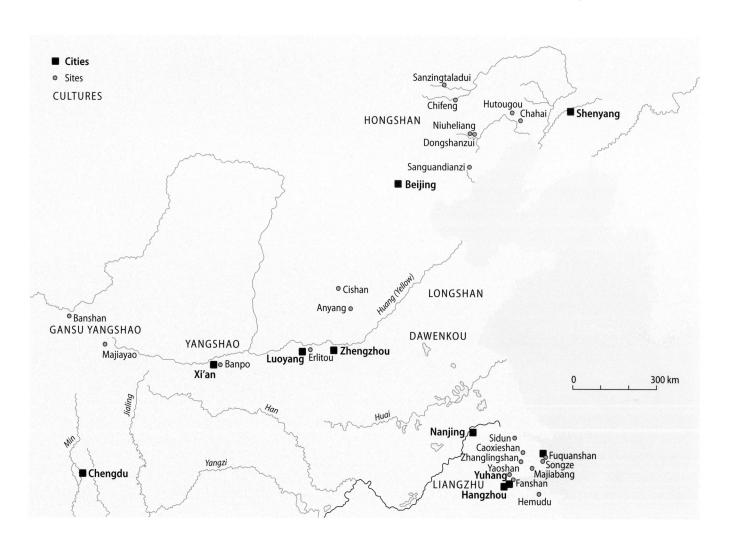

Fig 7 Jades in tomb 5Z1
Niuheliang site, Chaoyang City,
Liaoning Province
Hongshan culture (c 3500-2500 BC)

Jade was the principal, and often the only type of burial good used by the people of the Hongshan culture of north eastern China (c 3500-2500 BC), with many pieces found attached to garments or to the body.[1] The Hongshan people carved jade into the shapes of massive, strange, coiled monsters, sometimes referred to as pig-dragons, and also into bracelets and ornaments which were found near the head, chest, hands and feet in burials.

About 1,000 years after the Hongshan culture, and more than 1,500 km south in modern day southern Jiangsu and northern Zhejiang, large quantities of jades, including *cong* (tubes with a square cross-section and axial hole), *bi* (discs) and *yue* (axes), were placed in tombs around and on the body. These have been identified as belonging to what is now known as the Liangzhu culture (c 2500 BC). The *cong* are usually decorated with proto-monster mask designs at the four corners, indicated by eyes and parallel bars. These jades would have been time-consuming to produce, indicating owners of high social status. Their placement in tombs suggests that they were important components of the burial ceremony. Jades were probably also a form of protection, possibly against demons as seen in the later Han culture. A Liangzhu tomb could contain many more objects and in a wider range of sizes and weights than a Hongshan burial, indicating differences in use and presumably also in

Fig 8 Jade cong
Liangzhu culture (c 2500 BC)
Jade, 4.5 x 7.2 x 7.2 cm
Freer Gallery of Art

societal beliefs.[2] The later reuse of Liangzhu jades by other cultures was also common during ancient times, partly because the material was so precious and difficult to obtain.[3]

BRONZE AGE ANCESTOR WORSHIP AND THE AFTERLIFE

Ancestor worship was important to ancient Chinese people and still plays an important role in Chinese society today. People believed that their ancestors were guardians of the family who could communicate with the gods to bring them good fortune. They also believed that the afterlife was simply a continuation of this world, and buried their ancestors with objects for use after death, offering them food and wine in specially inscribed bronze vessels honouring the dead.

Bronze Age objects buried with the deceased show high levels of craftsmanship indicating their owner's importance. Chinese bronze pieces have been excavated from tombs, hoards and sometimes ceremonial pits, with the earliest being found in Erlitou (c 1900-1600 BC) near Luoyang, Henan. Chinese scholars have referred to the people of Erlitou as the Xia Dynasty, although there are only text records (*Shiji*) and no archaeological evidence to support the existence of such a dynasty. The Erlitou finds include both weapons and ritual vessels including three-legged wine cups, such as *jue* and *jia*. The cups were often less than half the size of weapons found in the same grave, indicating their relative importance to the Erlitou.

Jades were still valued during the Bronze Age and were still largely found in graves near the body of the deceased. Bronzes, including weapons, were found between the inner and outer coffins. Very different from the Greek bronze sculpture tradition, the Chinese cast their bronzes using piece moulds instead of hammering techniques, or by using the lost wax technique which was introduced to China in around the fifth century BC. Chariot fittings were produced to demonstrate their owners' social status, while mirrors and lamps were intended for everyday use in the afterlife.

SHANG DYNASTY
(C 1600-1050 BC)

The Shang Dynasty is the earliest in Chinese history whose existence has been supported by both archaeological and textual evidence. The Shang people lived in the Yellow River valley. They believed that their deceased ancestors, *Shangdi* or *di* (Supreme Deity), helped them to foretell the future through oracle bones. The ancestors sent signs in the form of cracks that appeared on a cattle scapula or turtle shell upon exposure to intense heat. Diviners interpreted the pattern of cracks and the prophecies read were carved into the bones. Later the bones were often buried in storage pits near the temple palaces.[4] Inscriptions on oracle bones and shells have helped archaeologists to identify the last nine kings of Shang.

The Shang made regular food and wine offerings to their ancestors using bronze ritual vessels. These vessels were kept in the family temple or shrine to be used by future generations, or buried in tombs for use in the afterlife and arranged in a specific order near to the coffin. However, jade was buried closest to the body of the deceased as it was believed to protect the body from demonic attack. Human sacrifice during funerals was also very common in this period; it was believed that social status and the obligation to serve should continue after death, and that the sacrificed people would serve the deceased.

By the Erligang period of the early Shang (c 1600-1400 BC), the types and styles of bronze ritual vessels had increased, mainly copying the shapes of ritual ceramics that had appeared in the earlier Neolithic period.

Fig 9 Oracle bone
Shang Dynasty (c 1600-1050 BC)
Tortoise plastron, 7.6 x 9.7 cm
Freer Gallery of Art

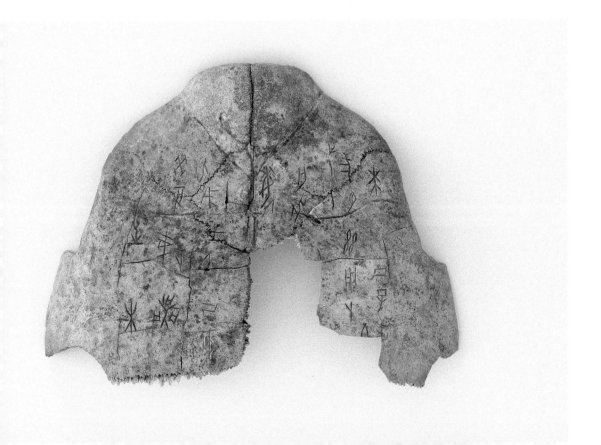

Fig 10 Bronze ritual vessel, *ding,* showing a *taotie* (or monster face) with large horns, big eyes and claws
Shang Dynasty (c 1600-1050 BC)
Bronze, 31.4 x 25 cm
Fitzwilliam Museum

The size and number of vessels in a grave indicated the owner's social status. For example, bronzes belonging to the Shang kings and their consorts are much larger and more varied in shape than those that belonged to members of the court. The most striking motif in Shang bronze decoration is known as a *taotie*, or monster face. There are many variations in the details of the monster's face on the bronzes, perhaps indicating that the designs were influenced by different patrons and times.[5]

Two other cultures in southern China – the Hunan and people from Guanghan Sanxingdui, Sichuan - were also interested in bronze and jade in this period, but the style of their work was rather different to the Shang's. Both cultures were unknown until archaeological excavations in the 1980s. Bronzes found in Hunan were cast as vessels in realistic animal shapes, instead of the hybrid creatures that have been found in the Shang region. Large bells were also popular in this area, but ritual vessels such as those found in the Shang capital, including *gu, jue* and *ding,* are hardly seen. This regional difference also applies to the people of Guanghan Sanxingdui in south-west China. Massive human-like bronze figures and heads (the largest is 2.61m tall), some of them even covered with gold foil, have been found in sacrificial pits. Although we have no idea how these bronzes were used during ritual ceremonies in these areas, the difference in their styles and scale may indicate a difference in religious practices.

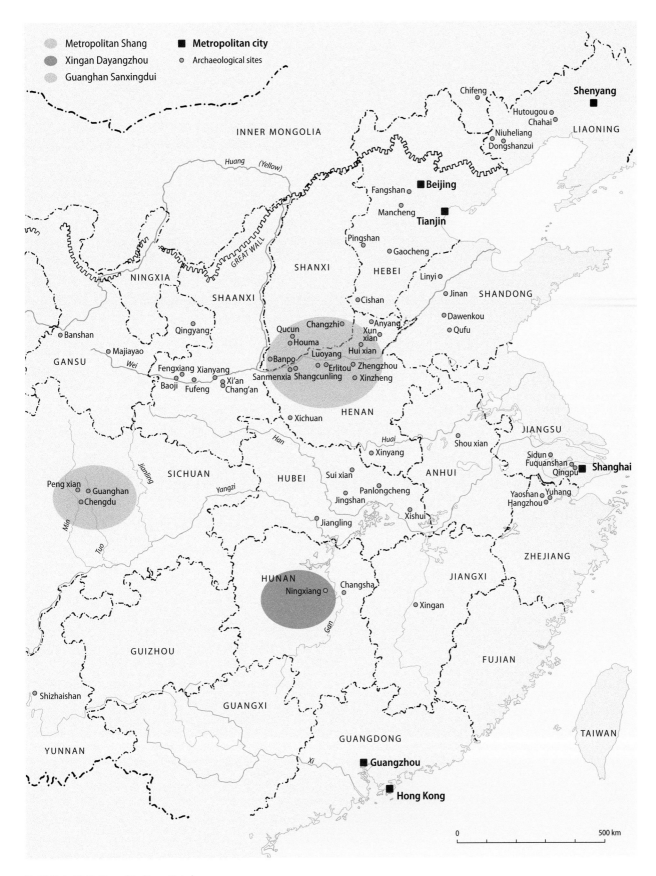

Legend:
- Metropolitan Shang
- Xingan Dayangzhou
- Guanghan Sanxingdui
- **Metropolitan city**
- Archaeological sites

INNER MONGOLIA

Huang (Yellow)

GREAT WALL

Chifeng
Hutougou
Chahai
Niuheliang
Dongshanzui

LIAONING

Shenyang

Fangshan
Mancheng
Beijing
Tianjin

Pingshan
Gaocheng

NINGXIA

SHANXI
HEBEI

SHAANXI

Cishan
Linyi
Jinan

SHANDONG

Banshan

Qingyang

Changzhi
Qucun
Houma
Anyang
Xun xian
Dawenkou
Qufu

Majiayao

Wei

GANSU

Fengxiang Xianyang
Baoji Fufeng
Xi'an Chang'an
Banpo
Sanmenxia Shangcunling
Luoyang
Erlitou
Hui xian
Zhengzhou
Xinzheng

HENAN

Xichuan

Han

Huai

Xinyang

Shou xian

JIANGSU

Peng xian
Guanghan
Chengdu

SICHUAN

HUBEI

Sui xian

ANHUI

Sidun
Fuquanshan
Qingpu

Shanghai

Jianling

Yangzi

Panlongcheng
Jingshan
Jiangling

Xishui

Yaoshan
Hangzhou
Yuhang

Min

Tuo

HUNAN

Ningxiang

Changsha

JIANGXI

ZHEJIANG

Xingan

GUIZHOU

Gan

Shizhaishan

GUANGXI

FUJIAN

YUNNAN

GUANGDONG

Xi

Guangzhou

Hong Kong

TAIWAN

0   500 km

Fig 11 Major Civilisations of the Shang Period

Jades were important in the burials of high-ranking individuals in each of these three areas. In the Shang region, 755 jades were buried near to the body of Fu Hao, consort of the Shang king, Wu Ding. They included ornaments, ritual vessels and trinkets in the form of two and three-dimensional animals. The jades found in Xingan Dayangzhou, Jiangxi were mainly ornaments and ritual vessels. Most of them (around 150 jades and almost 1,000 jade beads) along with some turquoise and crystal and a few bronze blades, were found inside the inner coffin of a high-ranking individual. Many of the beads and jades from the inner coffin are reminiscent of pendants or tassels.

Large jade blades, together with ivory tusks and the massive bronze figures mentioned previously, were found in two sacrificial pits at Guanghan Sanxingdui, Sichuan. It seems clear that these jade blades were used for ritual purposes although we are uncertain what that ritual involved. The jade collared discs and pointed blades are of a common design that was widespread across these regions, indicating that a certain degree of exchange of material may have taken place, despite their differing religious beliefs.[6]

WESTERN ZHOU DYNASTY
(C 1050-771 BC)

The origins of the Western Zhou people are still unknown, despite the existence of reliable documents and bronze inscriptions which help us to understand their history. The Zhou people had lived in the Wei River region of central Shaanxi Province towards the end of the Shang Dynasty, and later moved to settle at Qishan. In their earlier location the Zhou people must have already come into conflict with the Shang ruler, as the oracle bone inscriptions from Wu Ding's reign recorded expeditions against a people called Zhou.[7] The Zhou overthrew the Shang and founded a dynasty that lasted for eight centuries, with its power mainly concentrated in the Wei River basin in Shaanxi and the region on both sides of the Yellow River in southern Shanxi and north-western Henan.[8] After the conquest of the Shang, brothers and cousins of the Zhou king were rewarded with lands and titles. Consequently, ties between the Zhou ruling house and vassal kingdoms, which included the areas of modern Shaanxi, Shanxi, Henan and Shandong provinces, southern Hebei and northern Hubei, were very close at that time.

The rulers of Western Zhou believed in a spirit world, Heaven, rather than in the Shang's supreme deity, *Shangdi*. The Zhou sought to establish their legitimacy as rulers by claiming that the Shang kings had become less virtuous and therefore Heaven chose to withdraw its protection from them, conferring it instead on the house of Zhou. From that period onwards, the rulers of Zhou referred to themselves as *Tian Zi*, Son of Heaven. [9] Zhou rulers also practiced divination on a scale not known since the Shang Anyang court, with more than 15,000 oracle bones found in hoards in the palace at Zhou.

Before their conquest of the Shang in 1050 BC, the Western Zhou had already adopted Shang ritual vessel styles, however soon afterwards the Zhou added features to some of the bronze vessels to distinguish them from earlier Shang pieces. Square bases were added to raise the height of certain objects and to make them stand out among other ritual vessels, and decoration was added to give objects a spiky appearance. Realistic depictions of animals, such as buffalo that were possibly found in southern China at that time, were introduced. [10]

Bronze ritual vessels were an important feature of this period, and from the beginning of the Zhou Dynasty inscriptions were more common and often longer than in previous periods. These inscribed pieces have mainly been found in family shrines or temples, amongst hoards hurriedly buried during the invasion of the nomadic Quan Rong tribe from the west in 771 BC. They feature greater detail about important family members, family history and the history of the Zhou state, thus providing more accurate historical information than surviving texts. The inscriptions were cast on the inside and underside of the vessels, and were intended to be read by the family members who prepared the sacrifices and the ancestral spirits present. Bronze inscriptions from this period also record that the king sometimes made inspection tours to his vassal states and that his allies visited the royal house. In contrast, the majority of Shang bronzes were uninscribed or bear just the name of the owner, his family or clan and their ancestor's position within the ranks of the deceased. [11]

Fig 12 Bronze ritual vessel with inscription
Middle Western Zhou (late 10th-9th century BC)
Bronze, 40cm diameter
Fitzwilliam Museum

Fig 13 Set of seven bells
Late Western Zhou - early
Spring and Autumn Period
(mid 9th-mid 7th century BC)
Bronze, 20-41 cm x 8.5-21 cm
Shaanxi Institute of
Archaeology

In the middle of the Western Zhou Period (about ninth century BC), there was a restructuring of the royal government and a change in the way it related to society's leading families.[12] As a result, the typology of bronze ritual vessels became standardised into sets of identical *ding* and *gui* (cooking vessels and containers) in order to identify the social status of their owners. The small wine vessels, such as *jue* and *gu* that were popular in the previous period, disappeared and were replaced by pairs of large wine containers, *hu,* and sets of bells, possibly indicating changes to rituals and social structure. Motifs on the bronzes were simplified, probably because these ritual vessels were made for display in front of an audience that was less able to understand their significance. After the middle Western Zhou the use of inscriptions died out, suggesting that contact between the Zhou ruling house and the former Shang territories was broken, and with it had gone royal influence.[13]

Changes in society during this period are also reflected in the use of jade in burials. In the early Western Zhou the styles of jades were little different to those of the Shang Dynasty. However, between the late tenth and early ninth centuries BC, jade veils (jade stitched to fabric which was placed on the face of the deceased) and long pendants that consisted of jade, agate, faience and carnelian beads, started to appear in tombs of high ranking individuals in the regions of north and western China from where noble families originated. Gender differentiation can also be observed in burial items in terms of their shapes, colours and even materials. When the royal family moved their capital to the Luoyang area after the fall of the Western Zhou the use of the jade veil spread with them, but they were fewer in number and the material used was of an inferior quality.

In the period after the Zhou conquest of the Shang, ties between the vassal states and the royal house were strong. However, as time passed these kingdoms grew less dependent on the support of the Zhou ruling house, and their loyalty gradually faded away. In 771 BC, Quan Rong, the barbarian tribes allied with two of the King's vassals, invaded and killed the King. Although one of the King's sons was able to re-establish the Zhou court at the secondary capital at Luoyang, it did not command the power that the Western Zhou kings had enjoyed.[14] The Western Zhou Dynasty had effectively collapsed, fracturing into smaller states, and marking the start of the Eastern Zhou Period.

Fig 14 Ritual wine container with Zhong Jiang 中姜 inscription
Late Western Zhou to early Spring and Autumn Period (mid 9th century - mid 7th century BC)
Bronze, 53 x 17.8 x 13.8 cm
Shaanxi Institute of Archaeology

CHAPTER 2

WARRING STATES AND THE RISE OF THE QIN

James CS Lin

After the invasion by the Quan Rong from the north-west, the royal house of Zhou moved its capital to modern day Luoyang, which had previously been a Zhou stronghold in the east. This marked the beginning of the Eastern Zhou Period, of which the first 250 years are known as the Spring and Autumn Period (770-475 BC). Its title is taken from the chronicles of the state of Lu, the *Chun qiu* (The Spring and Autumn Annals), which covered the years 722-481 BC. The second part of the Eastern Zhou is commonly known as the Warring States Period (475-221 BC).[15]

During the Spring and Autumn Period, the Zhou territory was formed of 148 small states that were all related to the Zhou royal family. However, the more powerful states among them expanded their territories through warfare, bribery and political alliances, and extinguished neighbouring states, disintegrating the existing feudal structure. Wars continuously reduced the number of states, and eventually seven strong states

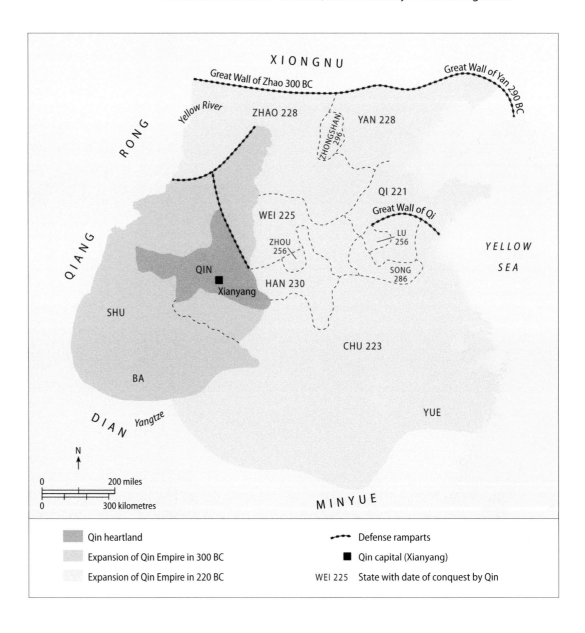

(previous page)
Detail of fig 30, *Bo* bell of Duke Wu of Qin

Fig 15 Map showing the states involved in the Warring States Period

Qin heartland

Expansion of Qin Empire in 300 BC

Expansion of Qin Empire in 220 BC

Defense ramparts

Qin capital (Xianyang)

WEI 225 State with date of conquest by Qin

Fig 16 Great Wall ruins
in Inner Mongolia

emerged during the late Warring States Period, each competing to unify China: the Han, Zhao, Wei, Chu, Yan, Qi and Qin.

The armies of the Spring and Autumn Period combined chariots with infantry; chariots were the preserve of the warrior aristocracy and the lower classes made up the infantry. The most important weapon for a noble on his chariot was the convex bow, while the infantry used lances. States' armies were small in scale at this time, with no more than 30,000 men, and battles usually lasted less than a day.[16] During the later Warring States Period the scale of battles expanded and military techniques improved. Armies came to rely on massed infantry and the use of cavalry increased. For defence purposes, each state built boundary walls along strategic points. Northern states, such as the Zhao, Yan and Qin, erected walls right along their state frontiers to defend against possible invasion by northern nomads. These walls were connected by the First Emperor after he unified China in 221 BC and formed the original 'Great Wall'.

The Warring States Period was an era of chaos and bloody battles, but it was also a golden age of Chinese philosophy. A broad range of thoughts and ideas were developed and discussed freely during this period. More than a hundred schools of thought evolved, but the most influential were Confucianism, Daoism, Legalism and the School of Yin-Yang. These thinkers were scholars, often employed by state rulers as advisers on methods of government, war and diplomacy. The Legalist philosophy adopted by the Qin pronounced that human nature was incorrigibly selfish and more inclined to do bad than good, and that the only way to preserve the social order was to impose discipline and strict law enforcement. The subsequent reform of the legal system conceived by the Qin statesman, Shang Yang (c 385-338 BC), which richly rewarded those who behaved well but severely punished wrong doers, laid the foundations for the Qin's unification of China. However, the concentration of power also hastened the collapse of the Empire after the death of the First Emperor.

Fig 17 Belt buckle with mandarin duck design
Spring and Autumn Period
(c 6th century BC)
Gold, 2.3 x 1.5 cm
Baoji Archaeology Institute

Fig 18 Chariot fitting with monster face design
Spring and Autumn Period
(c 6th century BC)
Gold with turquoise inlaid,
3.9 x 3.3 cm
Baoji Archaeology Institute

Fig 19 Chariot fittings in the shape of rabbits
Spring and Autumn Period
(771-476 BC)
Bronze, 5.7 x 2.2 cm
Longxian Museum

Fig 20 Soles of shoes
Spring and Autumn Period
(c 6th century BC)
Jade, 23.9 x 5.6-7.6 cm
Shaanxi History Museum

Fig 21 Belt buckle with duck design
Spring and Autumn Period
(c 5th century BC)
Gold, 1.2 x 2 cm
Shaanxi Institute of Archaeology

Fig 22 Bead necklace
Spring and Autumn Period (c 6th century BC)
Carnelian, 0.2-0.7 x 0.5-1.3 cm per bead (100 beads)
Baoji Institute of Archaeology

Fig 23 Arc-shaped pendant
Spring and Autumn Period (c 5th century BC)
Jade, 7.2 x 1.5 cm
Shaanxi Institute of Archaeology

Fig 24 Pendant
Spring and Autumn Period (771-476 BC)
Jade with carnelian beads, 7.1 cm
Longxian Museum

BURIAL PRACTICES IN THE WARRING STATES PERIOD

Although the Zhou kings continued to be the supreme universal leaders or 'Sons of Heaven' (*Tian Zi*) after they moved their capital to Luoyang, their political power gradually faded away, and after 500 years of conflict the Zhou monarchs' supremacy came to an end.[17] The further decline of the Zhou royal house in the Warring States Period meant that the bronze ritual sets that had been used in previous periods were no longer seen. Some were still found in tombs, but their appearance was less ornate, and a relatively new range of everyday bronzes such as lamps, braziers, incense burners and wine vessels appeared.[18] These items seem to have increased in importance compared to the ritual vessels that were used for ancestral offerings in earlier periods, partly due to new members of the elite being more interested in novel designs and exotic materials. Personal items, such as mirrors, belt hooks and even swords, were beautifully decorated and inlaid with gems. Gold items, which might have been introduced from the Steppes (the area beyond the Great Wall that stretched north and west into central Asia) started to appear in the elite tombs in the west. Lost wax casting techniques were also introduced to China, possibly from Europe through Central Asia, enabling the production of much more ornate decorations on bronzes, while gilt bronze became a fashion for the new elite.[19] Jade carving also reflected these changes in fashion, and new techniques such as open work jade became increasingly popular.

Evolution was also taking place in burial practices in terms of tomb structure and layout, grave goods and the way bodies were treated.

Fig 25 Tripod with lid
Warring States Period
(475-221 BC)
Bronze, 16.5 x 15.5 cm
Shaanxi Institute of Archaeology

Fig 26 Cocoon jar
Warring States Period
(475-221 BC)
Pottery with pigments,
36 x 13.4 cm (mouth),
33 x 22.5 x 10.4 cm (foot)
Shaanxi Institute of Archaeology

Fig 27 Horse-shaped
pottery vessel
Warring States Period (475-221 BC)
Ceramic, 16.7 cm
Shaanxi Institute of Archaeology

Fig 28 Hybrid creature with
exaggerated horns
Warring States Period (475-221 BC)
Gold, 11 x 11.5 cm
Shaanxi History Museum

Tombs in the southern regions, such as the Chu and Zeng states, were
similar to the houses of the living, and reflect the belief that the afterlife
was an extension of this world. The tombs were made up of several
rooms, identifiable from the objects placed inside them and through
descriptions recorded on bamboo slips.[20]

The materials placed inside tombs during the Warring States Period
show regional characteristics. For example, the use of crystal in pendants
was prevalent in the Shandong area, while lacquers and lost wax bronzes
were popular in the southern Chu region. Although jade has always
been China's favourite material, the types of jade objects differed from
area to area: the combination of jade pendants with carnelian beads was
commonly seen in western and central China, and might be a remnant
from the Western Zhou tradition. Similarly, jade discs were a phenomenon

of eastern China and may be related to the Neolithic Liangzhu jade discs that had earlier been used in this region. Tomb figurines became widespread during this period and were interpreted as substitutes for human sacrifices, however there are also regional differences here. For example, all figures from the southern Chu region were made of wood while most from the northern states were made from clay.

The southern practice during this period, of wrapping the body in silk, may have influenced the later development of full body coverings or jade suits. This custom, which combined the jade practice of eastern China with the silk system from the south, was also observed in the Western Han, where jade plaques were pasted onto silk and used to cover the bodies of Dou Wan and Nanyue Wang[21] (see page 123).

THE RISE OF THE QIN

The ancestors of the Qin state originated from the north-west border of China in modern-day Gansu Province. They were responsible for breeding and training horses for the Western Zhou's ruling kings (c 1050-771 BC). In 771 BC, their standing increased when Duke Xiang of Qin (r 777-766 BC) escorted the Zhou royal family eastwards from the Zhouyuan area to settle in Luoyang following the invasion of the Quan Rong tribe, leaving the Qin to guard the western frontier.

After taking over the regions abandoned by the Zhou, the Qin rulers took every opportunity to augment their power base, while being careful not to defy the Zhou ruling house openly. Instead, the Qin rulers remained allies of Zhou royalty through marital ties, and hosted the Zhou kings during their regular visits to their ancestral temples in Zhouyuan.

However, the Qin did demonstrate their great ambition by promoting themselves as the proxies of the Zhou royal house. The historian, Sima Qian, recorded in *Shiji* that the Duke of Qin performed a series of sacrificial activities which were the sole privilege of the Son of Heaven (ie the Zhou king), and inappropriate for a regional ruler.[22] A group of eight bronze bells, excavated from Taigongmiao near Baoji in 1978, confirm Sima Qian's observation of Qin ambition. These ritual bells were cast for Duke Wu of Qin (r 697-678 BC) and were indicative of power and social status. Their inscriptions, which reveal that he saw himself as having the 'Mandate of Heaven' and promising his successors a great future,[23] were meant to demonstrate the Duke's political ambitions to his officials, his guests and particularly his ancestors.

Further evidence of the Qin's ambition was revealed during the excavation of the tomb of Duke Jing of Qin (r 576-537 BC) and its contents

Fig 29 The tomb of the Duke Jing of Qin (r 576-537 BC), Nanzhihui, Fengxiang, Shaanxi Province

at Fengxiang, Shaanxi Province in 1986. The dukes and kings of Qin relocated their capital several times for strategic reasons, and their mausoleums were usually sited close by. Duke Jing of Qin's tomb is laid out according to the model of earlier tombs but on a greater scale. It is 300 metres long, 24 metres deep (equivalent to the height of an eight-storey building) and has two access ramps. Inside, 166 human sacrifices were buried alive to accompany the Duke into the afterlife, with pendants made of gold and turquoise beads found around some of their necks. At the bottom of the central pit (59 x 38 metres) there is a large wooden structure composed of several rooms linked by doors, like a living house, and a large number of real horses and chariots buried in a separate pit nearby. It is the largest pre-Qin burial found so far,[24] and shows that even in the afterlife the Duke of Qin competed with rival states in the rest of China. Although it had been looted several times in antiquity, more than 3,000 objects including gold, jade, bronze, bone, stone, pottery and lacquer were discovered, with exotic materials and designs indicating close trading links with the Steppe region.

The Wei River basin, which the Qin inherited from the Zhou ruling house, was the meeting point of Chinese and the Steppe region beyond. An important tomb was found there at Yimen, Baoji, Shaanxi, (c 550-500 BC) which is almost contemporary with Duke Jing of Qin, and is notable for the gold found within. It is a rectangular, vertical pit tomb that held an inner coffin which contained weapons and ornaments, and an outer coffin. Between the coffins there was a rectangular wooden box (*tou xiang*) that contained horse trappings. This tomb did not hold the bronze or pottery ritual vessels commonly seen in aristocratic Chinese tombs. Instead, it contained gold and iron daggers and a large number of gold ornaments such as rings, pendants and gold belt buckles, which are among the first known in China. Also found were beads of carnelian, turquoise and glass that may have come from central Asia, as well as jade plaques that possibly originated from the states of Chu or Wu in southern China. These exotic materials, and the preference for gold and iron rather than bronze, not only indicate that the tomb occupant was a high-ranking individual but also that they possibly came from the Steppes.[25]

The power of the Qin state reached its peak during the reign of Duke Mu (r 659-621 BC), particularly after his defeat of Duke Hui of Jin in 645 BC. At the same time, the Qin expanded their territory westwards, seizing land occupied by the Rong people. However, political turmoil in 441 BC, 425 BC and 385 BC weakened the Qin state.[26] Fortunately for the Qin, in 403 BC the most powerful state of the Spring and Autumn Period, the Jin, which had previously blocked the Qin's expansion eastwards, was broken up and divided between three major families; the Han, Zhao and Wei. This gave the Qin state a second chance to move eastwards, one which it took.

Fig 30 *Bo* bell of Duke Wu of Qin
7th century BC
Bronze, 64.2 x 22.4 x 26.2 cm
Baoji Bronze Museum

The Qin's military strength was enhanced under the guidance of Shang Yang (c 385-338 BC), a chancellor of Duke Xiao of Qin (r 381-338 BC). His numerous reforms included the transformation of the Qin's small armies, made up of aristocratic elite warriors mounted in light chariots, into large infantry-based armies of conscripted peasants, with a capitation (or head) tax introduced to fund the reforms. He instituted a system where one male was taken from each household to form an army squad of five, and soldiers were held responsible for each other's safety: if they lost one man it was their duty to capture the head of an enemy in exchange.[27] These groups worked in the fields during the busy growing season, and carried out military practice in their spare time. Shang Yang also organised families into groups of five, with members held legally accountable for each other's actions: failure to report a crime made the whole family culpable.

Before unification only aristocrats were permitted to hold rank and power, but the Qin created a system of ranks and grades that rewarded all men for success in battle. Success was measured by the number of decapitated heads of enemies taken; one head was rewarded with one rank, two heads with two ranks etc, and officers were given rank depending on the number of heads their subordinates removed. This strategy greatly motivated both officers and soldiers during the Warring States Period, and was maintained by successive Qin rulers after the deaths of Duke Xiao and Shang Yang.

While military and societal changes were being enacted, iron tools were also widely introduced, enhancing agriculture productivity, increasing food supplies and boosting the Qin's economic power. Although these developments occurred simultaneously in other states across the Warring States Period, the Qin took the best advantage of them. The reforms made by Shang Yang in 356 BC and 350 BC, assigning land to soldiers based upon their military successes and stripping land rights from nobility who did not fight, also encouraged the migration to and the cultivation of unsettled lands and wastelands. This standardisation of the land allocation system and reforms to taxation all helped to propel the Qin to prosperity.[28]

By the late Warring States Period, around 350 BC onwards, the Qin state had risen to a dominant position, conquering neighbouring kingdoms and expanding its territory in the process. Su Qin (380-284 BC), an influential political strategist, advocated the creation of an alliance of the eastern states against the state of Qin, but disputes among prospective allies undermined his plan. Zhang Yi (before 329-309 BC), another important strategist of that period, helped the Qin to dissolve the unity of its eastern opponents by suggesting that King Hui of Qin befriend the Wei and Yan states in order to break the alliance. This proved successful and paved the way for the Qin to unify China.

The turning point of the Qin's military campaign was the conquest of the Ba and Shu states in 316 BC. The natural resources of this region provided the invading Qin army with abundant food, and its location

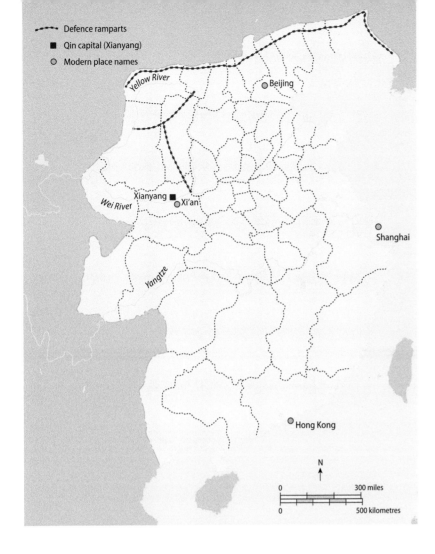

Fig 31 Map showing China at Qin unification in 221 BC

in the Sichuan basin provided the Qin with a perfect strategic position against its powerful neighbour, the Chu state. In 278 BC, Qin General Wu Qi defeated the Chu and captured its capital, and by 230 BC the Qin's military campaign and drive to unification had become unstoppable. In order to halt the Qin's invasion, several assassination attempts were made against King Zheng of Qin - the most famous of these is that of Jing Ke in 227 BC (see page 61) - however none were successful. There followed a period of conquest by Qin generals; from Governor Neishi Teng's defeat of the Han in 230 BC, to General Wang Jian's conquest of Qi in 221 BC. This culminated in 221 BC when Ying Zheng, King of the Qin, unified China and declared himself its First Emperor.[29]

The Qin had capitalised on the opportunity afforded by the Zhou's abandonment of the Wei River region, building a powerful state that lasted 505 years before eventually unifying China. That success was built not only on their ability to grasp opportunities and sheer luck, but also on wisdom and ambition. The Qin rulers were open minded, welcoming advisors from rival states, allowing them to climb to the top of the political ladder and even to engage in state reform. From Shang Yang to Wu Qi, and Zhang Yi to Li Si, many talented people from different states played crucial roles in the Qin's unification of China.[30]

CHAPTER 3

THE FIRST EMPEROR OF CHINA

XIUZHEN LI

The First Emperor of China, Ying Zheng, is one of the most controversial figures in Chinese history. He was born in 259 BC, first ruling as the King of the Qin Kingdom (246-221 BC), and later as the First Emperor (221-210 BC) of the unified Qin Empire. Regarded as a ruthless tyrant in the historical texts of Sima Qian (145-90 BC) and Jia Yi (200-168 BC), he has fascinated scholars for more than 2,000 years: as a unifier of China, as an innovator who laid the foundations of the Chinese imperial administrative system, as a seeker of immortality, but especially for the construction of his magnificent mausoleum and the Terracotta Army.

THE ORIGINS OF YING ZHENG

Before unification many kingdoms had attempted to ally themselves against the Qin's expansion, even undertaking unsuccessful assassination attempts. In order to divide and conquer such alliances the Qin sent some of their princes to these states as willing hostages; a move intended to help establish a mutual trust between their courts. Ying Zheng's father, Zichu, prince of Qin, was one such hostage in the Zhao state. Zichu was not treated well by the Zhao and was made to live in harsh conditions. However, he was able to meet a merchant, Lü Buwei, who was in the Zhao capital, Handan. Lü Buwei spotted potential in the young man and an opportunity, saying of Zichu: "This rare commodity should be invested in".[31] The cunning merchant convinced the childless Lady Huayang (the Crown Prince of Qin's primary spouse) to adopt Zichu as her son, establishing him as the heir of the Qin prince. Lü Buwei also helped Zichu to return to Qin, and gave Zichu his concubine. She gave birth to Ying Zheng, and with him was born the mystery of his parentage – was Zichu or the merchant his father? When Zichu ascended to the Qin throne as King Zhuangxiang, Lü Buwei was appointed chief chancellor and was made a marquis. Three years later, in 246 BC, King Zhuangxiang died, and Ying Zheng became King of the Qin at just 13 years of age. He too appointed Lü Buwei as his chancellor, but given the King's youth and inexperience the cunning ex-merchant effectively controlled the kingdom of Qin. This influence lasted for a decade until Ying Zheng, now 22, finally banished Lü Buwei and replaced him with another adviser, Li Si.

(previous page)
Fig 32 An imagined view of the E'Pang Palace
Yuan Yao (active c 1740-80)
Qing Dynasty, Qianlong Period
Ink and colour on silk,
172.6 x 127 cm
Museum of Fine Arts, Boston

Fig 33 Portrait of the First Emperor of China

With the assistance of his chancellor, Li Si, King Zheng carried out a series of reforms to radically develop agriculture and the Qin state's military capabilities. Through the skills of the officer, Meng Tian, the Qin increased the number of offensives waged against rival kingdoms – a strategy described as 'a silkworm devouring a mulberry leaf'[32] - and in the process grew more prosperous. By 221 BC, the six remaining kingdoms - Han, Zhao, Wei, Yan, Chu and Qi - had each been conquered and assimilated, the entire territory of what was then China had been united, and the first centralised empire had been established. This put an end to centuries of political turmoil, constant war and endless bloodshed between the so-called Warring States.[33] The Empire stretched from the east China coast to Lintao in the west, and from the Lang Mountains in the south to the Yalu River in the north. A tongue of territory even extended south into modern-day Vietnam.[34, 35]

Immediately after the unification of China in 221 BC, Ying Zheng proclaimed himself Qin Shi Huangdi. Ancient Chinese legends tell of three saintly sovereigns, *huang*, and five sage-rulers, *di*, so to reflect his supreme achievements and the unprecedented extent of his rule, Ying Zheng adopted a blend of the two names; *huangdi*. This was prefixed by *Qin*, the name of his 'native' kingdom, and *shi*, meaning 'the first', proclaiming the establishment of both an empire and a dynasty. Qin Shi Huang dreamed that the House of Qin might rule the Empire forever, and ordered that future rulers adopt a regnal number, ie the First, Second, Third Emperor and "so on for myriad generations".[36]

REFORMATION

In order to consolidate his newly built empire, the First Emperor set about enacting many political and technical reforms. The pyramid-like, hierarchical system that he created strongly reinforced the power of the central government and its political control over the new territories. The Emperor occupied the pinnacle while officials, graded in a series of ranks and paid accordingly, were appointed or dismissed by the Emperor on the basis of their merits and achievements. At the core of the new central government were the three Lords (*sangong*), comprising the prime minister (*chengxiang*), a military commander (*taiwei*), and the general supervisor (*yushidafu*). Below the three Lords were the nine ministers of state (*jiuqing*) who controlled specialist departments of government that looked after matters such as finance, criminal trials, palace security, command of the guards, the Emperor's horses and carriages, and affairs of the imperial family.[37]

However, the First Emperor held absolute power. For example, even the military commander did not have the power to raise forces or move troops without the consent of the Emperor, which was conferred using a bronze tiger tally. The tally was cast in two complementary parts, normally bearing inscriptions. The Emperor kept half of the tiger tally and the other half was given to the officer who controlled the military troops. Only when the Emperor sent his half of the tiger tally to the officer, who then matched the two halves together, could the officer legitimately move the troops.

In addition to creating new lords and ministers, the First Emperor of China abolished the old aristocratic and feudal structures and established a territory administration system known as commanderies (*jun*) and counties (*xian*). The whole Empire was divided into at least 36 commanderies, each of which comprised a number of constituent counties. Each county was further divided into a number of *ting*, and under each *ting* was a number of *li*, consisting of groups of individual families.[38] The commanderies and counties were governed by non-hereditary officials appointed by central government, and were supported in all cases by subordinate staff. As well as being a means of policing, this system also served to collect tax and maintain lines of communication.

The Qin officials in this hierarchical administrative system implemented strict laws, including statutes (*lü*) and ordinances (*ling*). The populace had to obey these written orders which were copied and circulated across the Empire. In 1975, the fortunate discovery of a set of these legal documents written on bamboo slips was discovered in a Qin tomb at Shuihudi in Yunmeng county, Hubei Province.[39] Each statute and ordinance bore its own title or number, and concerned a range of subjects including agriculture, craft production, the service of officials, labour conscriptions, and restrictions on convicted criminals.[40] Some of the provisions are concerned with the fine details of practical implementation, such as the delivery of official documents, security of government property and stores, rations for sentenced criminals, and even the use of lubricants for carts and carriages. One describes how when someone borrowed agricultural implements from government storage or weapons from the armoury, they had to be returned in line with the statutes, otherwise serious punishment would be inflicted. These bamboo slips provide a rare opportunity to see Qin laws and law enforcement in practice. One example reads:

> "When the quality (of manufactured objects) upon inspection is poor, the Master of Artisans [*gong shi*] is fined one suit of armour [*jia*], the Assistant [*cheng*] as well as the Head of the work-squad [caozhang] (are fined) one shield [*dun*] and the men (are fined) twenty sets of laces [*tuluozu*]".[41]

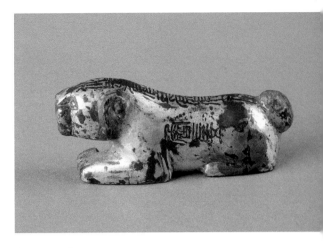

Fig 34 Tiger tally
Western Han Dynasty (2nd century BC)
Gilt bronze, 2.35 x 5.6 x 1 cm
Xianyang Museum

A controversial and very cruel measure adopted in 213 BC by the Emperor concerned book burning. The chancellor, Li Si, advised the First Emperor to burn all books of literature, with the exception of some on medicine and agriculture; a strategy intended to deprive people of learning, to suppress philosophies other than Legalism, and to control the population. Some Qin scholars criticised the central government, claiming that the move effectively restored old hierarchical systems based on rank. In the following year, criticism of the government became subject to severe punishment, and no fewer than 460 scholars were buried alive for voicing their opposition. Crown Prince Fu Su himself was sent away to command an army under General Meng Tian in punishment for his dissent.

ROAD NETWORK AND THE GREAT WALL

To improve transportation and communication links throughout his Empire, and to better control his vast territory, Qin Shi Huang built a road network. The first part, the speedway (*chidao*), was built in 220 BC and radiated eastward from Xianyang to today's Shandong, Hebei and the Liaodong Peninsula, southward to Hubei and Hunan, and south-east to Anhui, Jiangsu and Zhejing.[42] It was made for carriages and horses, with pedestrians separated from the main roadway by trees. The gauges of vehicles were standardised to smooth their passage along the carriageway. While the road system was built to aid transportation, at the same time official check points were established on mountain passes and at river crossings, with passage dependent on the presentation of wooden documents or certifications.[43]

In 212 BC, Qin Shi Huang ordered General Meng Tian to construct the second part of the road system, the Straight Road (*zhidao*). It carried horses and chariots from Yunyang (in present day Chunhua, Shaanxi Province) to Jiuyuang (in present day Jiuyuan, Inner Mongolia). The Straight Road was built to defend the Empire against the nomadic Xiongnu who raided the Qin Empire from beyond the border, and to allow commercial and cultural exchanges between the north and south of the country. Archaeological investigations were carried out in 2006 and 2010 to shed light on the Qin Straight Road's history,[44] and revealed chariot tracks and some footprints. Furthermore, four layers of rammed earth were found overlaid on one section of the Straight Road; the bottom one was the original Qin road, but the top layers were used during the Western Han and Eastern Han dynasties respectively, indicating that the Straight Road continued to be used after the fall of the Qin Dynasty. Even today, the Straight Road is still in good condition, indicating the solid construction of the rammed earth foundation.

A third Qin transportation project was the so-called Lingqu canal, built in the reign of the First Emperor but not recorded in contemporary literature. The canal was an ingenious achievement, cutting through

Fig 35 First Emperor burning books
and burying scholars alive
18th century
Painting on silk
Bibliothèque Nationale de France

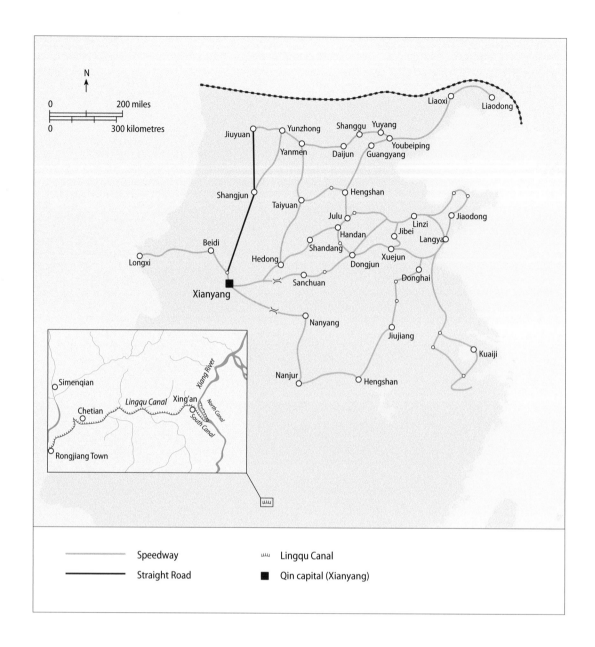

Fig 36 Map showing the speedway (*chidao*), the Straight Road (*zhidao*) and the Lingqu Canal

mountain ranges and connecting two rivers flowing in opposite directions; the southward flowing Lijiang River (a branch of the Zhujiang River) and the northward flowing Xiangjiang River (a branch of the Yangzi River in present day Guangxi Province).[45] The Lingqu canal served as both a transportation route and an agriculture irrigation system.[46]

As well as improving communications within the Qin Empire, the speedway and the Straight Road facilitated the rapid movement of troops against enemies from the north. In 215 BC, the First Emperor ordered General Meng Tian to march north into the Steppes with 300,000 soldiers to attack the Xiongnu nomads and to drive them out of their pastureland south of the Yellow River. At the same time, a line of defence, the Great Wall, was built to strengthen the Empire's new northern border; perhaps the best-known achievement of the First Emperor of China.

Fig 37 The Lingqu Canal
flowing through Xing'an,
Guangxi

In fact, General Meng Tian's wall was not the first to be built along the
northern border. During the Warring States era, Yan and Zhao, states
that had bordered the Xiongnu territory, built a series of interconnected
defensive walls. These earlier walls, sometimes made of stone and rubble
or compacted earth, were built for multiple functions:[47] for marking the
boundaries of a state's territories; preventing nomad invasion; collecting
tax from merchants crossing the border; observing the movement of
enemies, and for signalling or reporting to the Qin government officials
or military generals. Archaeologists have recently traced the lines of the
Qin and later Han Great Wall,[48] and have found the Qin Great Wall was
composed of three main sections: a western section of the Qin King's wall
along the western edge of the Yellow River, the northern section running
outside of the earlier Zhao walls (built in the Warring States era), and
an easternmost section parallel to the Yan walls and further south into
modern Korea.

After General Meng Tian had pushed the Xiongnu nomads back north of
the Yellow River, the First Emperor sent slaves and criminals to connect the
remaining walls by building new defences incorporating natural barriers to
form a continuous barricade. Thanks to a massive outlay of military, labour
and engineering effort, the Qin Great Wall eventually ran from Lintao
(in present day Gansu Province) in the west to Liaodong (in present day
Liaoning Province) in the east.[49] Exiles and commoners were relocated
to a new commandery, Jiuyuan, to cultivate the wild land along the

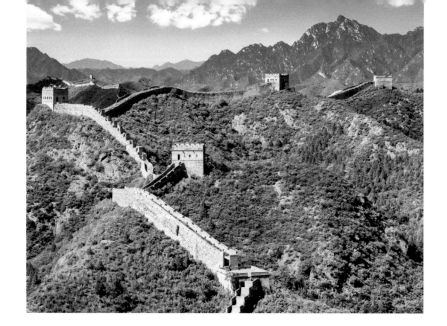

Fig 38 Ming Dynasty Great
Wall of China, Jinshanling
section near Beijing

northern frontier of the Qin Empire. Around 30,000 families, encouraged
by the reward of promotion in the hierarchy of honorary ranks, moved to
Beihe and Yuzhong along the Yellow River to defend the border.

The Great Wall came into its own shortly after the death of the First
Emperor in 210 BC. Fu Su, his eldest son, was forced to commit suicide, his
weak younger son was placed on the throne, and General Meng Tian was
executed, all of which precipitated the demise of the dynasty (see page
64). For several centuries thereafter, Xiongnu nomads launched assaults
against the Chinese,[50] but the Great Wall stood as a strong defence,
becoming "a source of great contention between the Steppe nomads and
the sedentary Chinese".[51]

STANDARDISATION
AND INNOVATIONS

Just as he had introduced political, legal and hierarchical changes
to the newly established empire, the First Emperor of China also
introduced innovations and standardisations to meet the demands of
ruling such a large territory and administration. The Emperor ordered the
standardisation of written characters, coins, weights and measures, some
right at the beginning of his reign in his early imperial decree of 221 BC.
These aided communication and trade in a large yet centralised empire.

The earliest example of Chinese written characters or symbols can be
traced to the Neolithic Period in the fourth or third millennium BC. The
later Shang Dynasty (1600–1050 BC) left evidence of a very complicated
system etched onto oracle bones (see page 23). In the Western Zhou

Period (1050-770 BC), the Chinese characters seen in bronze inscriptions, normally called large seal script (*dazhuan*), were added to the clay models or moulds, then cast on bronze vessels to tell the story of a single person or event related to the specific casting. Incised inscriptions were occasionally applied to the surface of bronze objects after casting using very hard, sharp tools. However, the upheavals of the Warring States Period (475-221 BC) brought political, economic and cultural changes, and variation appeared in the written characters of rival kingdoms. For instance, there were several different forms for the character 'horse' (*ma*) in the Qin, Qi, Chu and other states.[52] It was essential that official documents to the commanderies and counties in the unified empire were produced consistently and copied accurately, and so it became necessary to standardise the writing system. The First Emperor, advised by his chancellor, Li Si, adopted the small seal script (*xiaozhuan*), a simpler and more regular script, as the standard for the Qin Empire. Surviving Shuihudi documents from 359–217 BC, show this script had already come into use by this time for at least some official records. Another factor in the standardisation of writing was probably the increased use of the brush for writing.[53] Documents written with a brush onto silk, bamboo or wooden strips have been found from the fourth century BC, however scratching onto hard surfaces was more common at that time, making mistakes much harder to correct. As ink and a brush became more commonly used for daily writing, it became quicker and easier to copy documents and to correct mistakes by simply scraping off the ink using a small knife.[54]

Currency standardisation was not merely for economic convenience; it was also essential for the effective running of the imperial administration and was politically symbolic.[55] Before unification, a variety of different forms of currency, including cowries, tortoise shells, gold, silver and textiles, were used in different regions. The increased use of bronze by rival kingdoms during the Warring States era led to items such as spades, knives and small 'ant-nose' coins being cast to serve as currency. The Chu state

Fig 39 Coins including spades, knives, 'ant nose' coins and *banliang*
Warring States Period (475-221 BC)
Bronze
Emperor Qin Shihuang's Mausoleum Site Museum

Fig 40 *Banliang* coin mould
Warring States Period (475-221 BC)
Pottery, 16.6 x 8.5 cm
Qishan County Museum

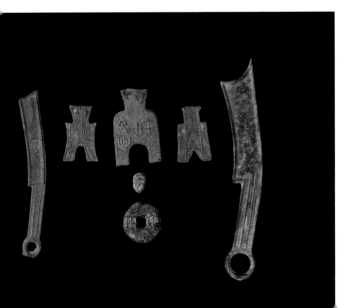

Fig 41 Bronze washer
Qin Dynasty (221-206 BC)
Bronze with gold and silver
inlay, 23 x 9.8 cm
Shaanxi History Museum

Fig 42 Measuring device
Qin Dynasty (221-206 BC)
Bronze, 27 x 5.5 cm
Shaanxi History Museum

Fig 43 Inscribed weight
Qin Dynasty (221-206 BC)
Pottery, 12.4 cm high, 2.85 kg
Shaanxi History Museum

(right)
Fig 44 Imperial edict
Qin Dynasty (221-206 BC)
Bronze, 14.1 x 7.7 cm
Shaanxi History Museum

had rich gold resources and introduced the gold currency, *yingyuan* or *chengyuan*, and sometimes ingots of gold were used by the upper classes.

The bronze, round coinage with a square hole in the middle was issued in 336 BC by the Qin state, and had a two-character inscription; *banliang*, translated as 'half-liang', where *liang* is a weight term (c 16 grams). Sometimes, a cord threaded through the hole could tie one hundred coins together for easy carrying. As the power of the Qin state had expanded, so had the use of the Qin coins, to the extent that this form of money was already in use in most of the conquered states on the establishment of the Qin Empire. The form of the Qin *banliang* remained the model for all imperial Chinese coins, right through to the Qing Dynasty (AD 1644–1912) and the end of the Chinese Empire.

Other changes during the reign of the First Emperor of China included the introduction of a unified set of weights and measures; a much harder standard to impose than other Qin innovations. The weights and measures used in the pre-Qin period varied considerably and were confusing to compare, so standardisation was not only very important for trade and tax collection but was also helpful for the Qin people's daily lives. In 221 BC, a short imperial edict was circulated, calling for compliance with the Qin Empire's new standards, and was even inscribed on the bronze plaques and everyday vessels seen in archaeological evidence. A bronze weight (*gaonu*) found in present day Gansu Province was inscribed with two edicts; one by the First Emperor (in 221 BC) which decreed that all weights be standardised, and another by the Second Emperor (in 210 BC) which called for compliance, reflecting the toughness and continuity of purpose on the matter during both emperors' reigns.

EMPEROR'S PALACES

Along with the Great Wall, the road network, the Lingqu canal and the famed mausoleum, the building of the Emperor's palaces was one of the largest construction projects in the Empire. The First Emperor was determined to manifest his power in monumental buildings, and the splendour of his palaces displayed the strength, wealth and advanced technical skill of the unified empire, effectively glorifying the political achievements of the supreme ruler. However, the construction of such structures needed a considerable investment in manpower and resources; a heavy burden on both society and empire, and one which may have contributed to the eventual collapse of the Qin Empire.[56]

After several relocations, the Qin capital was finally moved to Xianyang, about 12 miles north-west of present day Xi'an, in 350 BC by Duke Xiao. Under King Zhaoxiang (r 306-250 BC), Xianyang city gradually grew beyond its original confines, expanding out of the Xianyang Palace complex on the north bank of the Wei River. King Zhaoxiang had built new palaces on the south bank, accessible via a bridge, but further expansion was deemed necessary for the First Emperor. He expanded the city, transforming it from a mere state capital into the imperial centre of politics, commerce and culture.

In order to control the rich and powerful families of his conquered kingdoms, the Emperor ordered 120,000 influential families to relocate to Xianyang city, which both boosted the city's prosperity and kept these powerful families under surveillance. The Emperor also ordered the families to recreate the famous halls and palaces of their conquered kingdoms along the north bank of the Wei River. These probably included mansions, elevated walks and fenced pavilions, many filled with treasures and beautiful women captured from the other states. The buildings were

Fig 45 Hollow brick from
Xianyang Palace steps
Qin Dynasty (221-206 BC)
Pottery, 117 x 39 x 16.3 cm
Shaanxi History Museum

Fig 46 Large end ridge roof
tile with decorative *Kui* design
Qin Dynasty (221-206 BC)
Pottery, 37 x 51 cm
Shaanxi History Museum

linked to one another so that the First Emperor might walk among them and contemplate his many triumphs.[57]

The First Emperor later expanded the palaces on the south bank of the Wei River. The famous E'Pang Palace, started in 212 BC, was described in *Shiji* and noted for its grandeur and magnificence (see page 44). However, the lack of archaeological evidence for the palace suggests that it was not completed, so the much later *Shiji* reference is all we have.

Three years after the First Emperor's death, Xianyang fell to a rebel army. The invading general, Xiangyu, set the palaces alight and they burned for three months. From the remains and foundations, the architectural style and some decoration can still be discerned, particularly those of Xianyang Palace which was built on a high terrace and oriented north to south. Three palace foundations have been excavated by archaeologists, which revealed that the palaces were interconnected.[58] In the centre, above the terrace, was a two-story pavilion, surrounded by a cluster of other buildings connected by verandas and paved with hollow bricks decorated with dragons, phoenixes and geometric motifs. Some roof tiles with dragon, frog and deer designs were also found. The walls were plastered and painted with colourful murals or decorated with pictorial bricks. The floor was either painted or paved with bricks, underneath which lay a complete drainage system with linked ceramic pipes.

(clockwise from top left)

Fig 47 End ridge roof tile with stag and dog design
Qin Dynasty (221-206 BC)
Pottery, 26 cm diameter
Shaanxi Institute of Archaeology

Fig 48 End ridge roof tile with tiger design
Qin Dynasty (221-206 BC)
Pottery, 29 cm diameter
Shaanxi Institute of Archaeology

Fig 50 End ridge roof tile with dog design
Qin Dynasty (221-206 BC)
Pottery, 30 cm diameter
Shaanxi Institute of Archaeology

Fig 49 End ridge roof tile with leopard and rat design
Qin Dynasty (221-206 BC)
Pottery, 29 cm diameter
Shaanxi Institute of Archaeology

The main hall of the Xianyang Palace, where Ying Zheng lived before unification, was built on the top of a rammed earth terrace. An unsuccessful assassination attempt is thought to have taken place here in 227 BC. While the Qin state continued its unification plans, the Crown Prince of Yan, a small, weak state, plotted the assassination of King Zheng with a view to saving Yan. The Crown Prince sent Jing Ke to visit Qin, carrying with him a map scroll inside which a poisoned dagger was concealed. When the map was unrolled, Jing Ke seized the dagger, attacked Ying Zheng but missed his target, and so chased the King around his palace. King Zheng attempted to draw his own sword, but as it was a very long weapon was unable to do so. Other officials were not permitted to carry weapons in the Qin palace, so instead a royal alchemist threw his medicine bag towards Jing Ke to slow his chase, allowing the King to strike him in the thigh and stop him. Five years later the Yan state was conquered by the Qin.

Following unification, all weapons belonging to the conquered states were amassed in Xianyang and melted down to signify the permanent end of hostilities. To commemorate his conquest, the First Emperor had figures cast from the melted weaponry. It was recorded in *Shiji*: "Weapons from all over the Empire were confiscated, brought to the capital, Xianyang, and melted down to be used in casting twelve life-like figures standing in front of Xianyang Palace".

THE EMPEROR'S INSPECTION TOURS

Between 220 and 210 BC, Qin Shi Huang made five inspection tours of his domain,[59] and had seven inscribed stelae (stone tablets) erected on sacred mountains.[60] The tours had several objectives: to view the famous mountains and great streams of the Empire; to ascertain the adequacy of the Empire's border protection; to offer sacrifices to the cosmic spirits (fengshan); and to display the Emperor's presence and authority to his Empire.

The stelae inscription texts are valuable sources of information about Qin literature and ritual. The act of inscribing the stone was preceded by sacrifices to the cosmic power, and the inscriptions themselves commemorate the Emperor's visits and eulogise his unifying rule in contrast to the preceding ages of warfare and chaos. They proclaim that: "The Great Sage created his rule" and that he "established and fixed the rules and measures".[61]

Fig 51 First Emperor on tour in a palanquin
Chinese School (17th century)
Painting on silk
Bibliothèque Nationale de France

One year after his unification, in 220 BC, Qin Shi Huang embarked on his first inspection tour to the western border, including the commanderies of Longxi and Beidi (in present day Gansu and Ningxia provinces), from where his Qin ancestors came. This was partly to judge the security of the west frontier of the Qin Empire. In 215 BC, he went to the northern border in anticipation of a battle with the Xiongnu nomads, followed by tours to the eastern and southern parts of the Empire. In 219 BC, the First Emperor visited former kingdoms Qi and Chu, and performed *fengshan* (imperial sacrifices) at both the summit and the foot of the sacred Tai Mountain. The ancient Chinese rulers believed that they had a mandate from Heaven to rule on Earth, and offering sacrifices to Heaven or to cosmic spirits was a way to verify the legitimacy of their rule and the unification, and to receive blessings.

During his third tour in 218 BC, the First Emperor survived an assassination attempt in Wuyang (in present day Henan Province). The assassins hid amongst bushes along the mountain route and launched a very heavy piece of metal at the first carriage, assuming that the Emperor would be travelling inside and would be killed. Luckily for the First Emperor he was travelling in the second carriage.

On the way to Kuaiji Mountain (in present day Guangdong Province) in 211 BC, Qin Shi Huang visited the southern frontier of his realm and offered a sacrifice to the legendary ruler, Shun, who was believed to then be a mountain spirit residing on Jiuji Mountain (in present day Hunan Province). The inspection tour was not simply to see the mountains and streams, but was also to offer sacrifice in the hope of securing both his own and his Empire's immortality. The First Emperor conducted his fifth tour in 210 BC, again to the east, but died on the return journey, aged just 49.

THE DEATH OF THE FIRST EMPEROR

Qin Shi Huang was fearful of death, and searched for an elixir that would make him immortal. At the same time, he commissioned the building of his mausoleum at the foot of Li Mountain, 35 kilometres from the modern city of Xi'an.

During his second inspection tour in Shandong Peninsula in 219 BC, the First Emperor met a local alchemist, Xu Fu, who advised him that the elixir of immortality was to be found in the possession of the 'white-clad' immortal inhabitants of three divine or immortal islands, Penglai, Fangzhang and Yingzhou, in the Eastern Ocean. Xu Fu, together with

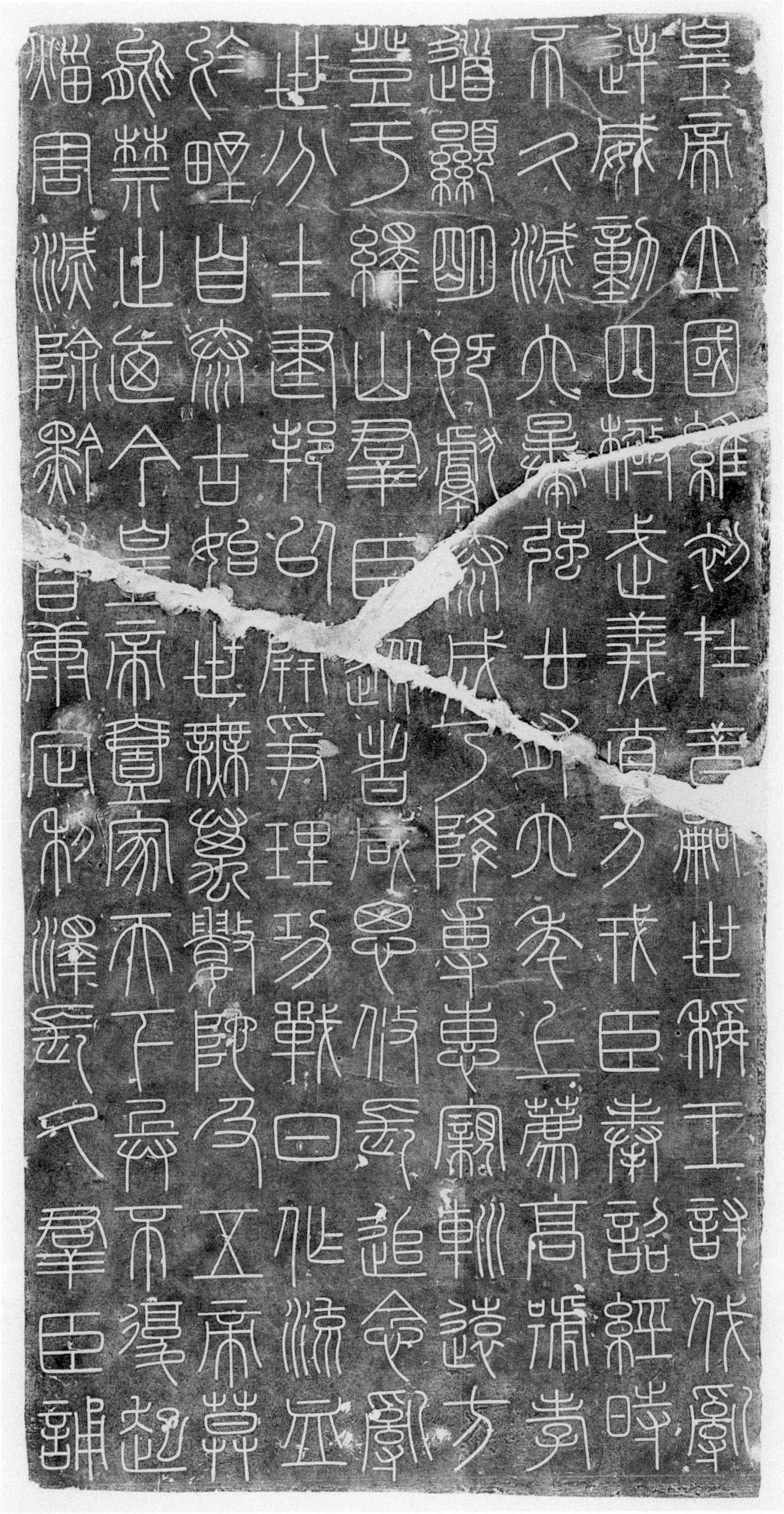

Fig 52 Inscriptions from the
stele of Mount Yi
Song Dynasty (960–1279)
Ink on paper (modern rubbing),
152.4 × 79.4 cm
Metropolitan Museum of
Modern Art, New York

Fig 53 The Immortal Islands
Chinese (17th century)
Watercolour on silk,
37.8 x 66.2 cm
Kupferstich-Kabinett,
Staatliche Kunstsammlungen,
Dresden

3,000 children and a small fleet, was sent on a mission to the Eastern Ocean to acquire the herbs and plants that could bring immortality. They never returned, and instead the Emperor ordered the palace alchemists to make potions which contained mercury in the hope it would extend his life, little realising that mercury is poisonous.

Those who accompanied the Emperor on his final inspection tour, particularly Zhao Gao and Li Si, concealed the news of his death and instead returned to Xianyang, each with the intention of naming a new emperor of their choosing before their opponents could wrest power. They had the Emperor's corpse concealed in the imperial chariot, and to mask the putrid stench in the summer heat they loaded a cart with salted fish to accompany the chariot back to the capital.

No record remains of the name of his empress, but the First Emperor had many concubines, and fathered many sons and daughters. Fu Su, as his eldest son, might well have had a strong claim to succeed him, but his criticism of his father's book burning (see page 50) had incurred the Emperor's anger, and Fu Su had been sent away to the northern border. Nevertheless, the Emperor had given orders suggesting that Fu Su should become his successor. However, Zhao Gao ignored these wishes, and through political manipulation engineered the accession of Hu Hai, a younger son of the Emperor with whom he had become friendly. Zhao Gao had overcome Hu Hai's misgivings about taking the throne and also persuaded Li Si, who was highly influential in the imperial court, to support his plot. Fu Su was forced to commit suicide while Zhao Gao also contrived the death of General Meng Tian, a man known for his military abilities and the construction of the Great Wall. He was also the man who had previously accused Zhao Gao of a crime which had resulted in a death sentence for Zhao Gao, one which was only commuted following the intervention of Ying Zheng, then King of the Qin. Zhao Gao had quickly advanced in the First Emperor's court and was with him on his last inspection tour, perfectly placed to take command of the situation and to capitalise on the Emperor's death.

No records show whether, once enthroned as Second Emperor, the 21-year old Hu Hai was able to take any personal part in governing the Empire. Instead he seems to have been manipulated by those around him who tried to profit from the situation, particularly Zhao Gao. Indeed, it may well have been Zhao Gao who forced Hu Hai to commit suicide in 207 BC.[62] After the suicide of the Second Emperor, Zhao Gao placed his own nominee, Ziying, on the throne, only to lose his own life soon after.

If a note of triumph marked the beginning of the Qin Dynasty, it ended in a state of weakness and a prevailing lack of purpose. The dynasty was short lived, and after Qin Shi Huang died it came to an abrupt end due to the influence of Zhao Gao and the weakness of the Second Emperor. Within just five years of the First Emperor's death, peasant rebels had stormed Xianyang and one of the leaders, Liu Bang, had taken the throne and established the Han Dynasty (206 BC – AD 220). However, in one way Qin Shi Huang did achieve the immortality and recognition he expected. In 209 BC, he was entombed in a magnificent mausoleum under the guard of his now world-famous Terracotta Army.

CHAPTER 4

THE TERRACOTTA WARRIORS

Xiuzhen Li

The life-size Terracotta Warriors, the legacy of the First Emperor of China, have deservedly become known as a wonder of the world. They were discovered in 1974, standing in haunting massed ranks in large pits, each warrior with its individual facial features. The three large warrior pits cover an area of 22,000 m², with the largest pit holding approximately 6,000 figures plus chariots and horses. However, these are only a fraction of his mausoleum complex, with around 600 pits and tombs found. The whole tomb complex covers approximately 56 km², making it nearly 200 times larger than the Valley of the Kings in Egypt, and comprises a central tomb mound surrounded by many kinds of ancillary tombs, pits and buildings used for services and sacrifices. The Emperor's warriors stand on the outskirts of the complex, some distance from the Emperor but ever ready to protect him and his underground empire.

Sima Qian recorded the construction of the mausoleum in *Shiji* but surprisingly did not reference the warriors themselves. In fact, no literary source gives a full account of the whole complex. Most of what we know about the mausoleum comes from the evidence revealed during archaeological surveys and excavations, however it is estimated that only 10% of the site has been unearthed over the past 40 years. This means that many secrets remain buried. The mausoleum itself remains unexcavated, but geophysical surveys and other technologies have been used to penetrate the mound.

(previous page)
Fig 54 Armoured infantry
Qin Dynasty (221-206 BC)
Terracotta, 179 cm
Emperor Qin Shihuang's Mausoleum
Site Museum

(opposite)
Fig 55 Middle-ranking officer
Qin Dynasty (221-206 BC)
Terracotta, 196 cm
Emperor Qin Shihuang's Mausoleum
Site Museum

(above)
Fig 56 Bronze chariot 2
Qin Dynasty (221-206 BC)
Bronze, 320 x 180 x 110 cm
Emperor Qin Shihuang's Mausoleum
Site Museum

Fig 57 Warriors after restoration

THE TOMB COMPLEX OF THE FIRST EMPEROR OF CHINA

Qin Shi Huang's dream that the House of Qin might rule the Empire for countless generations was over after just 15 years. However, after he died in 210 BC he was entombed in a magnificent mausoleum; a complex regarded as his afterlife universe.[63] Archaeological surveys and excavations have provided much evidence about the First Emperor's underground empire. In death, as in life, he had everything to continue his rule: a Terracotta Army to protect him; bronze chariots for travelling;[64] terracotta acrobats for his entertainment; an arsenal storing stone armour;[65] stables full of horse skeletons, and his concubines buried alive with him. Every individual included within the complex, whether human, animal or fabricated, had their role and duty to serve their Emperor. In one way, Qin Shi Huang did achieve the immortality and recognition he sought.[66]

What does the tomb complex tell us about the Qin Dynasty? How can we distinguish the natural, construction, ritual and burial landscapes? Can we understand the mausoleum's design and the changes made during construction? How did the First Emperor intend to rule in the other world?

A modern-day plan of the tomb complex hides several very different 'landscapes' that are related to different functions and activities that took place on the site,[67] each of which will be explored in this chapter. The natural landscape is concerned with the selection of the location for the Emperor's mausoleum based on *fengshui* theory. This process began after Ying Zheng ascended to the throne as the King of Qin, and would have continued once he became Emperor. The construction landscape was active from the moment the site was approved by the First Emperor and possibly earlier. Archaeologists have found evidence including kilns, stone workshops, road networks, tools, debris and the names and skeletons of the workers. The ritual and burial landscapes were designed into the plans of the Emperor's mausoleum. The ritual landscape was above the ground, with food and clothes being offered by the living to the dead Emperor in the halls in front of the tomb mound. The burial landscape was his underground empire, invisible to the living, but where he continued to rule in his afterlife.

NATURAL LANDSCAPE AND GEOMANCY

When he was just 13 years old (246 BC), shortly after becoming the King of Qin, the First Emperor started to plan his mausoleum. He chose a site that fitted traditional Chinese superstition about geomancy (divining from the land or soil) and *fengshui* (literally 'wind and water'), and at the same time developed his own understanding of his place in the cosmos. Siting the tomb was a very important issue for the ancient Chinese, and in one respect reflected people's beliefs about life and the afterlife. The First Emperor shared those commonly held beliefs and his tomb construction adhered to burial traditions, however he also expanded on and reinterpreted these legacies.

The First Emperor's mausoleum was a representation of his capital city, Xianyang, and was intended to provide a functional dwelling and even a universe in the afterlife. As outlined in the previous chapter, many of his Xianyang palaces were filled with splendid treasures and captured women, and while alive the Emperor walked amongst those buildings,

Fig 58 The tomb mound of the First Emperor

contemplating his triumphs. His tomb complex at Li Mountain was
intended to match Xianyang's immense size, opulence and lay out. Both
the dwellings for this life and the afterlife adhered to the ancient Chinese
theory of 'Yin' and 'Yang' which was widely used to explain natural and
social phenomenon. 'Yang' is male, and refers to the daytime, life, north
of the river and south of the mountain. 'Yin' is female, and refers to night
time, the afterlife, south of the river and north of the mountain. Xianyang
was located south of the Jiuzong Mountain and north of the Wei River,
and so was in an ideal site for living, while the Emperor's mausoleum was
north of the Li Mountain and south of the Wei River, a perfect location
for the afterlife.

The selection of an appropriate natural landscape was a priority not
only for the Emperor in his afterlife, but was also made for the benefit of

the countless Qin generations he expected to rule the Empire after him. According to the theory of *fengshui* (wind and water), energy rose from the mountain and was halted in its movement away by the water. To benefit from the energy of the landscape the First Emperor should locate his mausoleum on a south-north axis between the two geographical features and orientate his head towards the mountain and his feet towards the river. Subsequent emperors should then be buried on alternate sides of the First Emperor's mausoleum, between the mountain and river, so that the dynasty might benefit from the *fengshui* of the site.

However, the layout of the First Emperor's tomb complex does not seem to follow these rules. Archaeological evidence has shown that the mausoleum was east-west oriented, with the main gate and its tower and the main entrance to the coffin chamber both facing eastwards.[68,69]

Fig 59 A view of Pit 1

The Terracotta Army, buried in pits to the east, defends this precinct, facing towards the pass in the mountains through which the former state enemies might have been expected to come. From the point of *fengshui*, the First Emperor, as the ruler of the universe,[70] has occupied the whole area between the Li Mountain and Wei River, and has not left any space for future generations to share the energy. Archaeologists still argue about the reason behind this orientation of the mausoleum.[71] However, from a *fengshui* perspective, the lack of potential burial space on both the east and west sides of the Emperor's mausoleum was the reason for the rapid collapse of the Qin Dynasty.

LANDSCAPE IN CONSTRUCTION AND IMPERIAL LOGISTICS

In *Shiji*, Sima Qian provides relatively little information on the construction of the First Emperor's mausoleum, but does write that construction began shortly after he came to the throne as King of Qin in 246 BC. Any previous work probably involved location selection and design, and took place under the direction of Lü Buwei. Judging by the archaeological evidence, actual construction mainly started after the unification in 221 BC, continued into the reign of the Second Emperor and was interrupted by the peasant rebellion in 209 BC. This is supported by another account from Sima Qian: "about 700,000 labourers were conscripted to build the mausoleum after the unification". Some bronze weapons discovered in Pit 1 with the Terracotta Army also bear inscriptions indicating the year in which they were produced. The latest regnal year on the bronze lances is 228 BC, which indicates that the Terracotta Warriors were produced after this time.[72] Furthermore, a Qin standardised *banliang* coin was found in Pit 1, again pushing the construction date to after the unification.[73]

Between the Li Mountain and the Wei River was a perfect natural landscape for the burial site, however archaeological discoveries have shown some alterations were made to the land during the construction of the mausoleum. Before 246 BC, and probably before the unification, the landscape at the site of the tomb complex was mainly natural, with streams running through the Li Mountain slopes and trees and plants growing wildly. In order to protect the tomb mound and the underground coffin chamber, the courses of several streams were rerouted to the side of the mausoleum. Also, a large dam was built south of the tomb mound to prevent streams flooding the tomb complex.[74] This seems to have been successful as a geophysical survey showed that there was no water inside the tomb.[75] Preventing water from entering the chamber was described in Sima Qian's *Shiji*: "when the Emperor first came to the throne he began digging and shaping Li Mountain...

They dug down to the third layer of underground spring and poured in bronze to make the outer coffin resistant to the water". Other features were also added to the natural landscape during the construction of the mausoleum, including the artificial hill above the First Emperor's tomb called *Lishan* (which means Li Mountain).

Such a huge construction project was logistically complex, and involved administrators, overseers, craftspeople, labourers and even convicts who worked in iron handcuffs and shackles.[76] There were also craftspeople working in the workshops, labourers moving finished objects into burial pits or tombs, and supervisors overseeing on-site or from the top of the mountain. One hill summit on Li Mountain was levelled, with a local legend saying that the construction overseers built a platform there to control the labourers working across the site, beating drums to call the workers for breaks or meals. This area was and is still called Beating Drum Platform (*Jiguping*), and offers panoramic views of the enormous site. Some pieces of Qin ceramic were found by archaeologists on the platform,[77] confirming that it had a practical function.

The manual labourers working under the overseer were conscripted from all over the Empire. They worked day after day on the site - living, eating, sleeping and, in many cases, dying there. Some stamped or inscribed their names on roof tiles, bricks, pottery fragments and even on the Terracotta Warriors themselves. More than 90 names have been found on the backs of the warriors, including 12 stamped names, some of which are also seen on roof tiles and bricks.[78] These craftspeople probably worked in either the royal or governmental workshops before coming to the site for the mausoleum project.[79]

Several cemeteries of mausoleum builders were found within the complex. One of the cemeteries to the west of the mausoleum, near Zhaobeihu village, was found to contain many human skeletons buried in individual graves,[80] each one accompanied by a piece of pottery on which epitaph inscriptions were carved. Some of these people owed debts to the government and were forced to work for the mausoleum construction project rather than pay off what they owed. Others were recruited as forced labour. Some pottery inscriptions recorded the person's place of origin, their sentence or punishment, and their title and name, and also reveal how workers were mobilised from all over the country to work for the mausoleum project. These pottery records demonstrate that the huge administration required to run the site kept very careful records, but probably only for the skilled workers or commoners working on the site.

Another cemetery, found recently near Shanren village to the east of the Terracotta Warriors and the mausoleum, tells a quite different story.[81] Altogether 120 skeletons were found in a large burial pit, all male with one exception, and aged 15-35 years old when they died. They all seem to have died from natural causes, with no signs of violence. However, some seem to have been thrown into the pit, and some were obviously

Fig 60 Quality control marks inscribed onto
Terracotta Warriors
Qin Dynasty (221-206 BC)
Terracotta
Emperor Qin Shihuang's Mausoleum Site Museum

shackled with iron restraints. In contrast to the Zhaobeihu cemetery, the labourers here were buried without any sort of identification, suggesting a lower status, probably slaves or convicts. However, DNA test results from 19 samples have revealed far more variety in their origins.[82] The majority of the samples (53%) were from what is now southern China, with a further 37% from the north. However, one sample showed a closer genetic affinity with the ancestors of modern Japanese people, suggesting that the Qin government gathered slaves and convicts from the Empire and beyond.[83]

In such a complicated system, organisation was essential. Labourers worked for specific workshops in the construction landscape and each had their own tasks. The remains of several kinds of workshops have been discovered in the tomb complex. Kilns for firing roof tiles and bricks were mainly found to the west of the tomb mound, along the outer wall.[84] Several other kilns were found near the pits of the Terracotta Army, with some broken pieces of roof tiles and bricks inside but no evidence to show that they produced the terracotta figures themselves.[85] The raw material for all these pottery products was the local clay.[86]

A large stone workshop was found to the north-west of the mausoleum, with some iron tools, stone debris and iron shackles found on site. These hard labouring tasks were probably given to the convicted criminals, wearing shackles as they hammered stone. It is thought that another stone workshop was sited close to an abandoned Qin well at Xinfeng, to the north of the mausoleum. Many damaged and discarded stone plaques were discovered on the site and down the well itself.[87] These plaques were similar to the stone armour scales that were found at Pit 9801 (see page 127), with some bearing drilled holes to allow copper wire to pass through and link them together.

Fig 61 Bronze ritual vessel, *ding*
Qin Dynasty (221-206 BC)
Bronze, 61 x 71 cm
Emperor Qin Shihuang's
Mausoleum Site Museum

Labourers worked and moved among the workshops, completing their tasks before transporting the finished objects into the burial tombs and pits using carriages, carts or barrows. Road networks have been recently discovered within the tomb complex, with the footprints of workers and wheel tracks on the surface.[88] This ongoing archaeology may provide more detailed information on both the road network and the construction landscape as a whole.

Logistics were planned outside the construction site, but again happened on a very large scale. There must have been an overall leader, such as Li Si, who oversaw the whole project, as well as administrators and planners at the capital, Xianyang. There would also have been groups of people responsible for ordering and obtaining raw materials, such as the large quantities of timber needed as roof coverings for all ancillary pits, and the metals required for casting the bronze chariots, birds, bronze weapons and iron implements. Some objects were made on site, while other pieces were produced in the capital city or elsewhere and then transported to the tomb complex. The Wei River was also used to ship objects and materials, as it flowed directly between Xianyang and the mausoleum site.[89]

BURIAL AND RITUAL LANDSCAPES

The structures which would allow the First Emperor of China to live his eternal life in the complex were built thanks to the efforts of thousands of labourers, plus strong imperial logistical support. In contrast, the finished landscape would have been tranquil. The Emperor was settled in his underground empire – his burial landscape - but at the same time his spirit could ascend to ground level - the ritual landscape - to accept offerings from the living.

The burial landscape, which was and still is invisible to the living, comprised the underground structures for use by the First Emperor in the afterlife. His coffin chamber, regarded as his underground palace, was the centre of his underground empire. Sima Qian's account in *Shiji* says:

"Palaces, scenic towers, hundreds of officials, treasures and exotic objects, were brought to fill up the chamber. Craftspeople were ordered to set up crossbows on the sloping entrance, so that they could shoot down anyone attempting to break in. Flowing mercury was used to fashion the rivers, streams and seas in the Qin Empire. Above were set the heavenly bodies, with pearls and gems to symbolise the sun, moon and stars, and below were the features of the earth. 'Man-fish' oil was used for lamps, which were calculated to burn for a long time without going out. Concubines without any children were all buried with him".[90]

However, details of the vast burial landscape, including the large number of ancillary tombs and pits, were not recorded in *Shiji*.

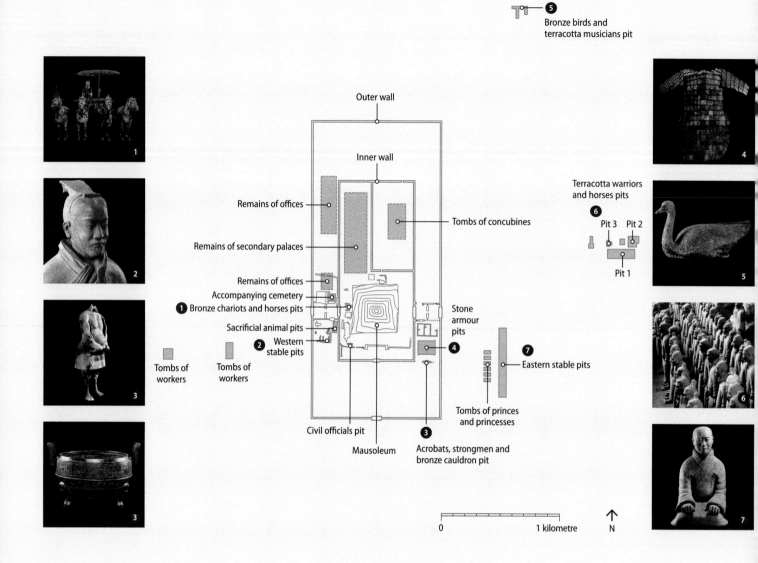

Fig 62　Plan of the Emperor's burial site

As described, the mausoleum itself has not been excavated, however other methods have been employed to explore it. Geophysical surveys of the inside of the tomb mound have shown an earthen terrace structure with towers and steps above the coffin chamber, assumed to have been to allow the Emperor's spirit to come up to view his land and to accept offerings.[91] Within the inner and outer walls were structures for the daily rituals required to sustain the Emperor in the afterlife. A small palace-like building was placed behind the mound to the north-west. This building, called *qindian*, housed the imperial gowns, caps and staff, and here food and wine offerings were provided for the Emperor's spirit. A secondary

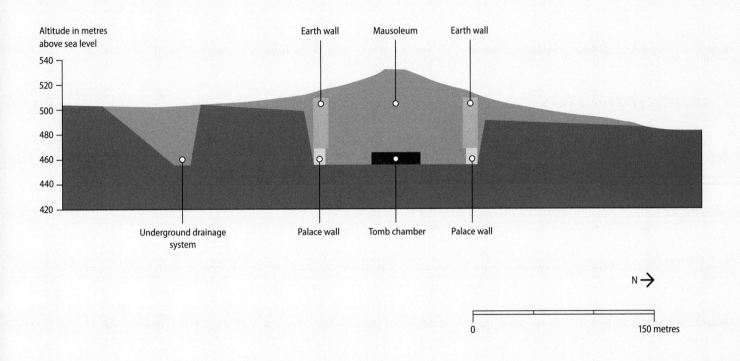

Altitude in metres
above sea level

540
520
500
480
460
440
420

Earth wall   Mausoleum   Earth wall

Underground drainage
system

Palace wall   Tomb chamber   Palace wall

N →

0   150 metres

Fig 63 Cross section of the
First Emperor's mausoleum

ritual building, called *biandian*, located to the north-west of the *qindian*
within the inner wall, was the residence of the large numbers of servants
and ritual officials. Within the west section of the outer wall was a building
called *shiguan*, or provisioning office. This was the special department
in his ritual landscape for preparing food and drink for the spirit of the
deceased Emperor. Ceramic containers and fragments have been found
here, including the pottery lid of a vessel bearing the inscription '*Lishan
shiguan*'.[92] Lishan is 'Li Mountain' but also refers to the First Emperor's tomb.

FINDS FROM THE BURIAL SITE

The builders of the complex were anxious to protect the secrets of the tomb, so when the mausoleum construction approached its conclusion many labourers who had worked to arrange the treasures inside the coffin chamber were sealed inside while alive to avoid them revealing the secrets to the outside world. Also, the mausoleum was covered with vegetation: "trees and bushes decorated the slopes, giving the mound the appearance of a real mountain". This would have prevented the relatively loose earth from sliding down the slopes,[93] as well as hiding the secrets within.

Archaeological surveys and excavations, conducted since the Terracotta Army was discovered in 1974, have shed much light on the whole area. However, interpreting recent archaeological discoveries in the First Emperor's tomb complex has been a challenge for historians, archaeologists, anthropologists and archaeological scientists. We know that the mausoleum was a replica of his regime or life, and so the First Emperor brought everything he would need to meet his living, ruling, travelling and entertaining needs, but what did the individual pits of the tomb represent? What was their specific function in his afterlife?

The two walls encircling the tomb mound and his underground palace symbolise the inner and outer courts of the palaces of the living. The objects found within the walls were probably very important to the Emperor's daily life. These included bronze chariots, concubine tombs, exotic birds and animals, an arsenal, acrobats, stables and Pit K0006 containing terracotta figures, a wooden chariot, bronze axes and horse skeletons.[94] The two exquisite bronze chariots, half the size of the originals, were buried in a wooden chamber, 20 metres west of the tomb mound. Their most conspicuous feature is their very faithful reproduction of every single component in bronze, gold and silver.[95] A variety of techniques, including casting, soldering, hammering and drilling were employed to make the chariots and the gold and silver inlay and ornaments. Their miniature size emphasised their exquisite character and importance in the service of the Emperor, and it is highly likely that they were for the Emperor's afterlife journeys, with inspection tours of his territories probably being the most important afterlife trips he intended to take. For such tours, horses had the same importance as chariots, partly because so many following officials, generals and servants would ride them.

Horses were very important to the Qin society, not only because their ancestors raised horses for the Zhou Kings, but also because they were essential for transportation and military purposes. During the Emperor's lifetime, his highly valued horses were well treated and used to draw his chariot or carry generals into battle. Many Qin stables' names were recorded in *Shiji*, on Qin bamboo slips,[96] and even carved on the pottery

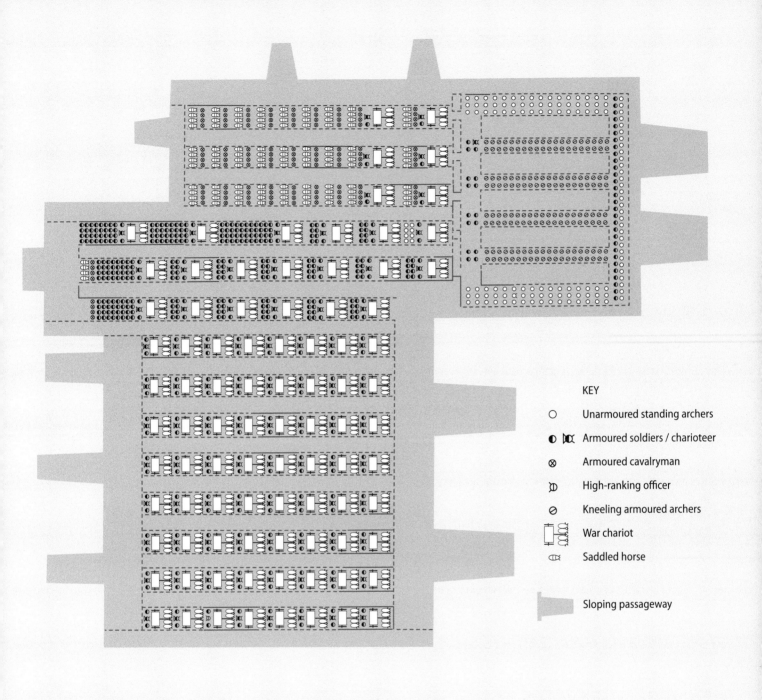

vessels found in the mausoleum complex.[97] Their names include '*dajiu*', '*zhongjiu*', '*xiaojiu*', '*gongjiu*' and '*zuojiu*', and denote Qin stables for horses with different purposes. Many horse skeletons were discovered both within and outside the tomb complex walls. Some highly valued horses were found in the coffin, while others were buried in a single pit with the terracotta figure of a stable boy to look after them.

Pit K0006, found to the south of the tomb mound, contained more than 20 horse skeletons and twelve terracotta figures (four charioteers and eight others) but their purpose is not entirely clear. Did this pit represent

Fig 65 General
Qin Dynasty (221-206 BC)
Terracotta, 198 cm
Emperor Qin Shihuang's
Mausoleum Site Museum

Fig 66 Plan of Pit 2 showing the position of cavalry and infantry units and chariots

Fig 67 Terracotta Warriors
and horses

Fig 68 Stable boy
Qin Dynasty (221-206 BC)
Terracotta, 68 cm
Emperor Qin Shihuang's
Mausoleum Site Museum

the Qin court, or *tingwei*,[98] or possibly one of the Qin royal stables?[99] Were the charioteers and horses intended to escort the First Emperor on daily or long-distance travelling?[100] If these terracotta figures do symbolise court officials why are there four charioteers and more than 20 horse skeletons in the court?

Eight figures in Pit K0006 were found wearing flat headgear and long robes with hands hidden by sleeves resting in front of their bellies. They are similar to those discovered in other pits, just to the west and between the inner and outer walls, in which horses were buried in coffins.[101] Each coffin contained three horses, with a knife in the mouth of one of the horses indicating that the horse was killed before burial.[102] The four bronze axes found in the pit were probably for preparing hay for horses rather than simply ceremonial objects representing justice and equality. They are similar to iron axes found in other pits of stables within the tomb complex.[103]

The quantity and variety of horse skeletons found with their terracotta stable boys and stable hands indicates their importance in the First Emperor's daily life. Evidence has been found which suggests that he also wanted rare animals and birds in his private garden. Pottery coffins containing the bones of animals and birds, as well as clay dishes for food, were found to the west of the mausoleum. On either side of the coffins were pits containing kneeling pottery figures, presumably keepers. The animals and birds may have been rare specimens acquired as gifts and kept in the imperial garden or the vast imperial hunting park, *shanglinyuan*.[104]

Recent discoveries in the north-east section of the inner city are thought to be the burial sites of the First Emperor's concubines. An archaeological survey found a cemetery, comprising about 99 ancillary tombs, close to the tomb mound. A trial excavation of 19 tombs found them all to contain female skeletons of relatively young ages, with a delicate pearl necklace found on an access ramp.[105] These tombs' locations and the all-female skeletons tally with Sima Qian's account that the Emperor's childless concubines were buried alive with him by the Second Emperor. This also indicates that the mausoleum design changed during construction, as this decision was made by the Second Emperor after the death of his father.

(previous page)
Fig 69 Cavalry horse
Qin Dynasty (221-206 BC)
Terracotta, 175 x 215 cm
Emperor Qin Shihuang's
Mausoleum Site Museum

Fig 70 Bronze chariots and horses being excavated

Fig 71 Pottery coffin
Qin Dynasty (221-206 BC)
Pottery, 98.8 x 59.2 cm
Emperor Qin Shihuang's
Mausoleum Site Museum

Fig 72 Bell with gold and
silver inlay
Qin Dynasty (221-206 BC)
Bronze, 13.14 cm
Emperor Qin Shihuang's
Mausoleum Site Museum

Fig 73 Helmet
Qin Dynasty (221-206 BC)
Limestone, 38 x 21 cm
Shaanxi Institute of Archaeology

Fig 74 Armour
Qin Dynasty (221-206 BC)
Limestone, 99 x 75 cm
Shaanxi Institute of Archaeology

Fig 75 Musical instrument,
chunyu, with a tiger on top
Qin Dynasty (221-206 BC)
Bronze, 48.6 cm
Shaanxi History Museum

(opposite, top)
Fig 76 Tiger detail from fig 75

Fig 77 Garlic head wine container
Qin Dynasty (221-206 BC)
Bronze, 38 x 20.5 cm
Shaanxi Institute of Archaeology

Stone armour and helmets were stored in the arsenal, Pit K9801, of the Qin underground empire, adjacent to the Emperor's palace. The arsenal was intended to provide for the spirits of soldiers who died in the conquering wars of unification.[106] A suit of horse armour was also found in the trial trenches, which demonstrates a need to protect the horses in war.

Entertaining was also one of the themes for the First Emperor's afterlife. A pit adjacent to the tomb itself contained a group of terracotta figures of performers in moving postures, mostly wearing just skirts. A massive figure stands with his hands held in front of him. Another, much more slender entertainer has a hand raised with a finger pointing up to the sky.[107] A major difference between these figures and the stable men and the warriors is the sense of movement conveyed. Their lifelike gestures and diverse bodies, ranging from very slender to heavy and muscular, are very different to the impassive stable men and the immobility of most of the warriors. It is apparent that the craftsmen of the Qin Dynasty could readily achieve a sense of movement, but only rarely was such individual realism required. It is evident that at each site different features were emphasised according to the functions required.

The terracotta figures with bronze waterfowl found in Pit K0007 depict another form of entertainment. These figures, 15 in all, were posed as if playing music, while in front of them a group of waterfowl, including charming swans, elegant cranes and wild geese in lines, are ready to dance to the music in a clear stream. One kneeling figure seems to hold a mallet in his right hand, which is raised high in the air as though striking a bell or a drum, while his left hand rests on his left thigh. The bronze birds are laid in neat order along the riverbanks. Each bird is unique and well depicted in bronze, and even birds of the same species are slightly different to each other. One of the bronze cranes is holding a little worm in its beak; the creature frozen at the moment when the crane plucked it from the water.[108] No one can help but be surprised by this impressive scene, only meant for the First Emperor of China's afterlife.

THE MAKING OF THE TERRACOTTA WARRIORS

People are fascinated by the Terracotta Warriors; almost 8,000 life-size figures, each weighing between 110 and 300 kilos and measuring about 1.8 metres in height. They are thought to stand guard over the Emperor, and are equipped with lethal bronze weapons and are placed into battle formation. They stand to the east of the First Emperor's mausoleum, buried in three pits, and include infantry, cavalry, charioteers, archers and crossbowmen. The army headquarters is even represented. To date, more than 40,000 bronze weapons have been found in the partially excavated area, including swords, lances, halberds, spears, dagger-axes, hooks, arrows, crossbow triggers and ceremonial weapons, *su*, which were also placed into the battle formation. The Terracotta Warriors and weapons provide a rare opportunity to investigate the Qin society, military, arts and technology in China's first established empire.

The making of the Terracotta Warriors was initially thought to be a process combining moulding and detailed sculpting.[109] However, Ledderose (2000)[110] proposed that the makers used more of a mould and mass production system. He suggested that several types of heads, torsos, arms, hands, legs, feet and even plinths were produced individually, and then assembled into different combinations. Recent collaborative research between the Emperor Qin Shi Huang's Mausoleum Site Museum and University College London's Institute of Archaeology, has shown that the Terracotta Warriors exhibit far greater individuality than simply assembling limited numbers of each body part would produce.[111,112]

Fig 78 Goose
Qin Dynasty (221-206 BC)
Bronze, 57 x 27 cm
Emperor Qin Shihuang's
Mausoleum Site Museum

Fig 79 A digital recreation of water birds sitting alongside the artificial river found in Pit K0007 in the mausoleum site

Fig 80 Charioteer
Qin Dynasty (221-206 BC)
Terracotta, 191 cm
Emperor Qin Shihuang's
Mausoleum Site Museum

Fig 81 Standing archer
Qin Dynasty (221-206 BC)
Terracotta, 184 cm
Emperor Qin Shihuang's
Mausoleum Site Museum

Fig 82 Terracotta Warrior heads

The Terracotta Warriors bear the stamps or carved names of their makers, including administrative, artistic and technological leaders as well as foremen. They both organised and created individual terracotta figures, and stamped or incised their names on a specific part of the body to indicate their input. For example, most stamped names, *gong* (meaning 'palace' in English) plus craftspeople's names were seen at the bottom of the robe, while some incised names, *Xianyang* (capital of the Qin), were found in the armpits or on the back of the Terracotta Warriors, again alongside craftspeople's names. Each figure normally bears one name, stamped or carved.[113] If each warrior was made by simply assembling different body parts we might expect to see finished figures with several names on them – one attached to each body part. However, this is not the case for most of the finished Terracotta Warriors.

Further research focused on the ears of the terracotta figures. Human ears are very distinctive from each other, and sometimes serve almost as a finger print in criminal investigations. Many photographs were taken of ears in the Terracotta Warrior pits and then 3D versions were generated using specialist software, showing the precise features of each ear. More than 30 photographed ears show high levels of individuality in their detailed sculpting, suggesting that they were completely hand produced rather than mould cast in several types.[114]

The clay used to produce the Terracotta Warriors was made from local loess, probably with sand added during the shaping process.[115] Each Terracotta Warrior body was built from the ground upwards in a succession of body parts made from thick coils of clay, while its head was made and fired separately, with soft clay used to fill any gaps between the head and body. A considerable amount of sculptural detail, including robes, scale armour, hair and facial features, was then added by hand to the basic human form, before the clay figure was dried in the shade and fired in a huge kiln for several hours at a temperature between 950 and 1050°C. From a logistical point of view, it seems likely that most or all of these manufacturing steps occurred in close spatial proximity to one another, as well as near to the clay sources, kilns and pits.[116] After firing, each Terracotta Warrior was covered with lacquer before various bright pigments were applied.[117] They were then placed in their military formation in the pit and equipped with their weapons.

The Terracotta Warriors' weapons were mostly made from bronze, with only one iron spear head and five iron arrow tangs fitted with bronze arrow heads found. As described earlier, it is recorded in *Shiji* that after unification bronze weapons from all over the Empire, including the Qin's own, were confiscated and melted down to be used in casting bells, bell stands and twelve bronze men to stand in front of the palace.[118] However,

Fig 83 Warriors being conserved

the archaeological evidence suggests that this was not the case, as large quantities of Qin bronze weapons have been found in the Emperor's tomb complex. Some of the weapons, particularly the bronze lances and halberds, bear long inscriptions to indicate the regnal year in which they were produced, the name of the person in charge of production, the official or workshop, and the name of the specific worker, thus providing basic information on both the chronology and the organisation of production during their manufacture. It would also allow the maker's work to be properly scrutinised,[119] and so was essentially a form of quality control. According to the inscriptions carved on the bronze lances and halberds, these were mainly produced from 244-228 BC, during the reign of King Ying Zheng but before the unification,[120] and had possibly been used before entering the tomb complex. The Prime Minister, Lü Buwei, appears as the supervisor of the halberds' production, but not of the lances': all of the halberds were produced before that date, and the lances afterwards. The fact that the Prime Minister was inscribed as supervisor on the halberds indicates a strong degree of political control over the production of weapons. However, the following Prime Minister, Li Si, does not appear as supervisor in the later lances, suggesting changes in the

organisation of production, possibly related to political changes during the Qin era.

In contrast, the arrows and the crossbow triggers seem unlikely to have been used before being buried with the Terracotta Warriors. Approximately 300 bundles of arrows (each bundle comprising about 100 arrows) and more than 10,000 loose arrows were found in the Terracotta Army trial trenches.[121] Observational and chemical analysis suggest a high level of consistency within each bundle and variability between bundles,[122] which indicates that these bundle arrows had never been used in the battle field and were specifically produced for the First Emperor's afterlife.

More than 200 crossbow triggers were found with the Terracotta Army. The introduction of the crossbow revolutionised military warfare,[123] permitting the archer to fire heavier arrows (bolts or quarrels) more accurately, with greater force and penetrating power, and over a longer distance than regular bows. These bronze trigger mechanisms were made in three separate parts with two pins and then assembled.[124] Each part had to be precisely cast and filed smooth in order to be assembled properly and to function effectively.[125]

Fig 84 Modern recreation of the warrior construction process Shaanxi Promotion Centre

Fig 85 Kneeling archer
Qin Dynasty (221-206 BC)
Terracotta, 122 cm
Emperor Qin Shihuang's
Mausoleum Site Museum

Remarkably, the arrows and some other weapons produced specifically for the First Emperor's Terracotta Army were sharpened as for the Qin's real troops and were lethal. The polishing marks on each piece are very fine and parallel; a feat that was difficult to achieve without a rotary wheel or other mechanical device. The polishing and sharpening of more than 40,000 bronze arrows in workshops with lathes must have been done on an industrial scale.[126]

In 209 BC, the year the Second Emperor came to the throne, the builders, craftspeople and convicts who had worked on the mausoleum were equipped with weapons, some probably from the Terracotta Army, to fight the peasant rebellions. Many of them died, and like those buried

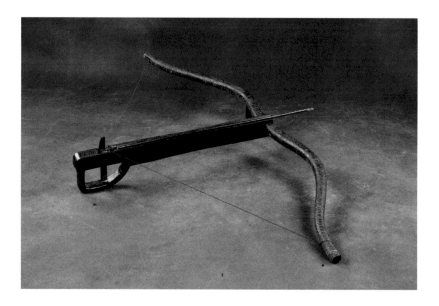

Fig 86 Replica of a crossbow
143 x 86 cm
Emperor Qin Shihuang's
Mausoleum Site Museum

Fig 87 Crossbow mechanism
Qin Dynasty (221-206 BC)
Bronze, 16 cm
Emperor Qin Shihuang's
Mausoleum Site Museum

alive in the mausoleum took the secrets of the First Emperor's tomb complex to their own graves. The trees and grass that grew on the top of the site also contributed to its secrecy, to the extent that following the collapse of the Qin Dynasty and the rise of the Han Dynasty, no one remembered that the silent clay army stood ready to protect the First Emperor's eternal life.

Fig 88 Arrowheads
Qin Dynasty (221-206 BC)
Bronze, 11.3 - 13 cm
Emperor Qin Shihuang's
Mausoleum Site Museum

Fig 89 Dagger-axe
Warring States Period
(475-221 BC)
Bronze, 25 cm
Shaanxi History Museum

Fig 90 Spearhead
Qin Dynasty (221-206 BC)
Bronze, 19.3 cm
Emperor Qin Shihuang's
Mausoleum Site Museum

(overleaf)
Fig 91 Rows of warriors

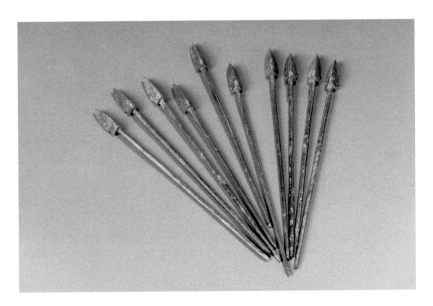

CHAPTER 5

HAN ROYAL TOMBS

JAMES CS LIN

After the death of Qin Shi Huang in 210 BC, peasant uprisings erupted throughout the country and civil war ensued. The popular revolt was finally quelled in 206 BC, and Liu Bang was proclaimed the new emperor of the Han Dynasty. The Han Dynasty lasted for more than 400 years and rivalled the almost contemporary but smaller Roman Empire in the west; an AD 2 census records almost 60 million people in the Chinese Empire. The first half of the dynasty (206 BC-AD 8), is known as the Western Han. After a short interregnum under Wang Mang (AD 9-25), the Han Dynasty re-established itself at Luoyang, and the subsequent period is known as the Eastern Han (AD 25-220). It is considered a golden age in Chinese history.

THE STORY OF THE HAN

The history of the Han Dynasty (206 BC-AD 220) is recorded in several scripts including the *Shiji*, compiled by the Han historian, Sima Qian (146-86 BC). To corroborate this textual evidence, we have a wealth of archaeological material from innumerable sites throughout the country, which provides reliable information about Han history, economy, society and their thoughts about the afterlife.

The Han Empire was divided into areas directly controlled by the central government using an innovation inherited from the Qin Dynasty known as commanderies. The majority of eastern China was divided into semi-autonomous kingdoms that were given to generals who had helped Liu Bang to unify China. However, the Emperor feared that this would again lead to China being split into several independent kingdoms, and so contrived to kill or exile the non-Liu kings and instead installed his sons and relatives in their places. Gradually the vassal kingdoms lost all vestiges of their independence, particularly after the failed rebellion of the Seven Kingdoms in 154 BC, and China was unified again.

The Xiongnu, a nomadic Steppe tribe on the northern border of China, had always threatened the Han Empire. It succeeded in defeating the Han in 200 BC and forced them to submit as a *de facto* inferior partner, while continuing their raids on the Han borders. Emperor Wudi (156-87 BC) launched several military campaigns against them and eventually divided the Xiongnu into two separate groupings. He expanded the Han territory into the Tarim Basin of Central Asia, which helped to establish the trade network known as the Silk Route.

When Emperor Ping died (r AD 1-5), his relative Ruzi Ying was chosen as the heir and Wang Mang was appointed to serve as regent to the child. Despite promising to relinquish control to Ruzi Ying once he came of

(previous page)
Fig 92 Painted soldier figure from the Han general's tomb at Yangjiawan
Han Dynasty (c 2nd century BC)
Terracotta, 48 x 15 cm
Xianyang Museum, Xi'an

Fig 93 Portrait of Han Gaozu Liu Bang (r 206-195 BC), founder of the Han Dynasty (c 2nd century BC)
Chinese School, (18th century)
Vellum
British Library

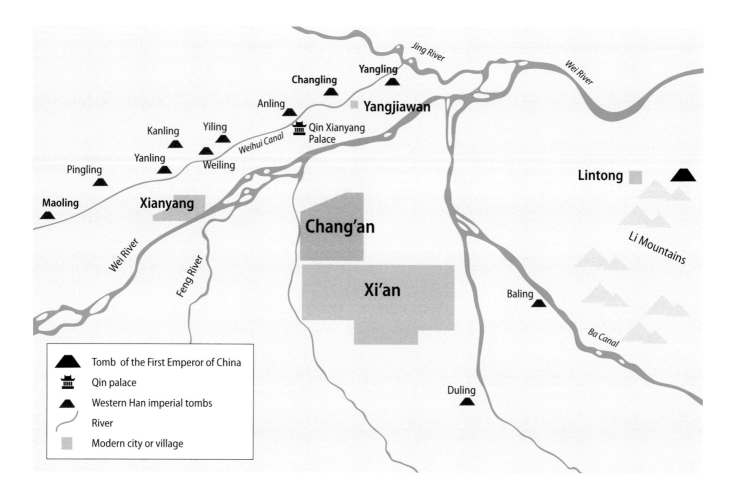

Fig 94 Locations of Western Han emperors' mausoleums

age, and in the face of protests and revolts from the nobility, Wang Mang instead claimed to have the divine Mandate of Heaven and began his own dynasty, the Xin (AD 9-23). Like the founder of every new dynasty, Wang Mang initiated a series of major reforms, including introducing new currencies and nationalising land for equal distribution between households. However, the reforms were ultimately unsuccessful, and the problems were compounded by extensive flooding between AD 3 and AD 11 which caused a large number of peasants to rebel.

Liu Xuan, King of Huaiyang, a distant descendant of the Han Emperor Jing (r 157-141 BC), attempted to restore the Han Dynasty and occupied Chang'an as his capital. However, he was overwhelmed by rebels who replaced him with a puppet monarch, Liu Penzi. Liu Xuan's brother, Liu Xiu, was urged to succeed him as emperor and successfully established the separate Eastern Han Dynasty, taking the title of Emperor Guangwu (r AD 25-57).

Foreign travellers to Eastern Han China became more frequent during this period; the opening of the Silk Route allowed better communication with the outside world, establishing cultural and trade links. As its power and influence grew so did diplomatic ties, and gifts were exchanged. Consequently exotic, luxury objects were found in royal tombs and Chinese materials were found along the Silk Route.

Han emperors during the Eastern Han Period did not usually live long, and their sons succeeded to the throne when they were teenagers if not younger. Their youth and inexperience gave the empresses and their relatives, and even court eunuchs, the opportunity to take control in the court. After AD 92, palace eunuchs succeeded in gaining power, engaging in court politics with various consort clans of the empresses and the empress dowagers. Their political manoeuvrings eventually led to rebellion and ultimately to the collapse of the Han Empire.

EMPEROR JING'S MAUSOLEUM

Like the Qin Dynasty before them, the Han understood the afterlife to be a continuation of this world, and constructed mausoleums for their emperors that met their everyday and spiritual needs. Most of the emperors of the Western Han Dynasty chose the Xianyang highland as

Fig 95 Portrait of Emperor Jing (157-141 BC), the fourth emperor of the Han Dynasty

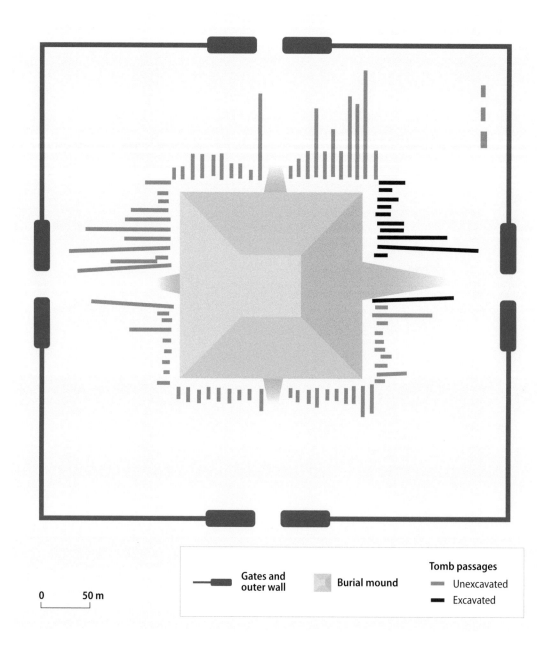

Fig 96 Tomb layout of Emperor Jing at Yangling

Gates and outer wall

Burial mound

Tomb passages

Unexcavated

Excavated

0   50 m

their eternal resting place as it is situated just to the north of the ancient Han capital, Chang'an, at a distance that was ideal for future sacrifices by their descendants and for the management of the mausoleums. None of the Han emperors' tombs were excavated during the twentieth century and most, if not all, were looted in earlier times.[127] Following recent surveys we know that they were designed, like the First Emperor's burial, as underground cities.[128]

The burial site of Jingdi, the fourth emperor of Han (r 156-141 BC), was discovered when an airport expressway was constructed at Han Yangling. It is a pyramid-shaped mound with 81 tomb passages of differing lengths that lead to the main burial chamber. Ten of the passages to the north-

(clockwise from top left)

Fig 97 Armoured figures excavated from Emperor Jing's tomb at Yangling, Shaanxi Province

Fig 98 Excavation of ceramic livestock figures in no.13 secondary burial pit at Emperor Jing's tomb at Yangling, Shaanxi Province

Fig 99 Excavation of ceramic goats and sheep in Emperor Jing's tomb at Yangling, Shaanxi Province

100

103

101

104

102

105

Fig 100 Rooster painted
with pigments
Han Dynasty (c 2nd century BC)
Pottery, 15.5 x 15 x 6 cm
Han Jingdi Yangling Museum

Fig 101 Dog painted
with pigments
Han Dynasty (c 2nd century BC)
Pottery, 35 x 19.9 x 9.2 cm
Han Jingdi Yangling Museum

Fig 102 Piglet painted with pigments
Han Dynasty (c 2nd century BC)
Pottery, 16 x 7 cm
Han Jingdi Yangling Museum

Fig 103 Goat painted with pigments
Han Dynasty (c 2nd century BC)
Pottery, 38.5 x 28.3 x 12.3 cm
Han Jingdi Yangling Museum

Fig 104 Calf painted
with pigments
Han Dynasty (c 2nd century BC)
Pottery, 72.8 x 38 x 23.5 cm
Han Jingdi Yangling Museum

Fig 105 Horse figure
Han Dynasty (c 2nd century BC)
Pottery, 70 x 59.5 x 18 cm
Han Jingdi Yangling Museum

west of the tomb were excavated in 1998 and found to contain tens of thousands of ceramic animals and figurines, both male and female, as well as weapons, horse and chariot decorations, bronze and clay seals, storage jars and food containers that were prepared for the Emperor's afterlife. Every passage had a door through which burial objects could pass into the main tomb. Judging from the inscriptions on the seals and the contents of these tomb passages, it can be concluded that these passages were meant to represent different departments and institutes of the central government of the Western Han Dynasty. Such a tomb plan was clearly intended to create a complete world for the dead Emperor.[129]

Unlike the Terracotta Warriors, the beautiful figurines contained in Jingdi's tomb are less than half-size. Also unlike the warriors, they are made with moveable limbs, are painted and were carefully dressed in silk clothing that has now decayed. However, they follow in the same tradition as the warriors and were intended to function as servants and guardians of the Emperor in the afterlife.

During his 17-year reign, Emperor Jing suppressed the rebellion of the Seven Kingdom's in the east and secured the centralisation of his government. Afterwards, his son, Liu Sheng, was installed as the first king of Zhongshan kingdom in modern Hebei Province, and his Grand Commandant, Zhou Yafu, who had helped him to put down the rebellion, was promoted to Prime Minister.[130] Both of their tombs were excavated in the 1960s and both offer rare glimpses into the royal tombs of that era.

Tomb of a Han General

More than 3,000 items, including 1,965 warriors, 583 cavalrymen and 410 shields were accidently discovered by farmers in 1965 at Yangjiawan, 25 km east of Xianyang city. The warriors and horses symbolised infantrymen and cavalrymen, while other soldiers represented ceremonial guards, clerks and commanders. The objects belonged to a nearby tomb, M4, the occupant of which has been identified as a high-ranking military official; either Zhou Bo or his son, Zhou Yafu, the general who had helped Emperor Jing to suppress the Seven Kingdoms.

The actual tomb mound stood 70 metres away. It is rectangular in shape, has a long tomb passage with a 90-degree turn, a sacrificial pit in front of the tomb chamber, and three pits for utensils near the entrance of the tomb passage. A horse and chariot pit was found in the tomb passage and another two outside the tomb. A consort was also buried nearby in tomb M5. Both tombs had been seriously looted and damaged, and only a small number of bronzes, lacquerware and chariot fittings survived. However, around 200 jade plaques were found inside M4, with traces of corrosion on the plaques suggesting that they were sewn with silver thread to form a jade suit.

Fig 106 Naked male figure (originally with movable arms and dressed in silk) Han Dynasty (c 2nd century BC) Pottery, 56.7 x 9.3 cm Han Jingdi Yangling Museum

We know from *Shiji* that General Zhou Bo died in 169 BC and his son, Zhou Yafu, in about 154 BC. Shortly before their deaths, both were charged and found guilty of rebellion.[131] When Zhou Yafu tried to explain that the 500 sets of armour and shields bought from the imperial workshop were for his mausoleum rather than for a revolt, the commandant of justice commented: "perhaps you did not intend to revolt in this world but only in the world below?"[132] This story emphasises the Han belief in the afterlife as a continuation of the mortal world.[133]

(Also fig 108 overleaf)
Fig 107 Painted soldier figures
from the Han general's tomb at
Yangjiawan
Han Dynasty (c 2nd century BC)
Terracotta, various sizes
Xianyang Museum, Xi'an

ROYAL TOMBS
IN EASTERN CHINA

Even today it is forbidden to open the tombs of Chinese emperors, so our understanding of Han tombs and their structures is based on the tombs of royal family members in the eastern kingdoms. These were excavated in the 1980s and 90s, prior to the start of construction projects or as rescue excavations after tomb looting.

Most of the Liu family members' tombs have been found in areas that belonged to the powerful kingdoms of Lu, Liang, Zhongshan and Chu. These tombs were carved horizontally into rocky mountains, with long tomb passages leading to different chambers; very different to the vertical pit tombs used in earlier periods.

In May and August 1968, the first two complete jade suits ever found were excavated at Mancheng county, Hebei Province. Tomb M1 belonged to Liu Sheng, the son of Han Emperor Jing and an elder half-brother of Han Emperor Wu, as well as the first king of Zhongshan kingdom (established 154 BC).[134] M2 belonged to his consort, Dou Wan, who is not mentioned in historical texts but her name is known from a bronze seal found in her tomb. Judging from the inscriptions on the 'Eternal Fidelity' palace lamp found in Dou Wan's main coffin chamber she may have been a relative of Empress Dowager Dou (Dou Taihuo), mother of Emperor Jing.

These two royal tombs are particularly important, not only because they belonged to people who were closely related to Emperor Jing, but also because few intact Han tombs have survived to help us understand the original arrangement and function of their tomb chambers. The tombs were sited on the east slope of Lingshan Mountain, M1 to the south of M2, and about 120 metres apart. Each was carved into the rocky mountain and included six chambers that served different functions in the afterlife.

In Liu Sheng's tomb, the right-hand chamber was a storage room, filled with various types of ceramic vessels, wine containers and a millstone, and with a dead horse in close proximity. The chamber on the opposite side of the entrance passage held a tile-roofed, wooden-framed building, with four chariots and eleven horse skeletons inside. This chamber was certainly a stable.[135] The central chamber was occupied by two tents, an array of large bronze vessels, a row of lamps, incense burners and 19 figurines (18 of which were made from clay). Behind the tents were placed an array of bronze drinking cups, a miniature chariot and a pile of coins. The abundant cooking and drinking vessels, containers and model servants suggest that this central chamber in Liu Sheng's tomb was a place for a ritual banquet; a ceremonial chamber.[136] In front of the rear chamber there was a thick stone gate blocking the entrance. Four large

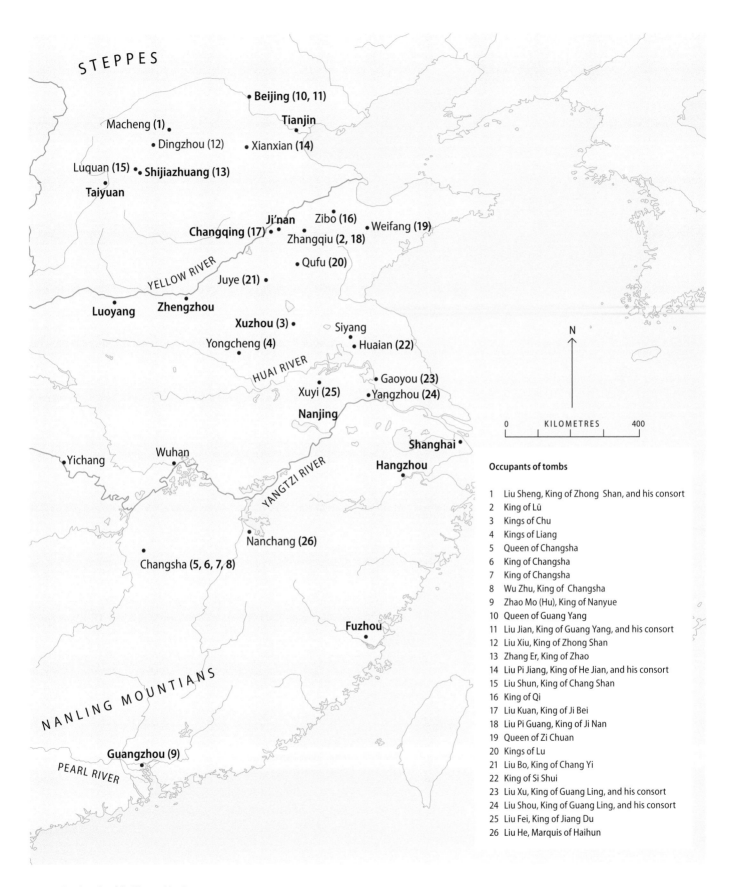

STEPPES

• Beijing (10, 11)

Macheng (1) •
Tianjin

• Dingzhou (12)   • Xianxian (14)

Luquan (15) • • Shijiazhuang (13)

Taiyuan

Ji'nan   Zibo (16)
Changqing (17) •   • Weifang (19)
Zhangqiu (2, 18)

• Qufu (20)

YELLOW RIVER   Juye (21) •

Luoyang   Zhengzhou

Xuzhou (3) •   • Siyang

Yongcheng (4) •   • Huaian (22)

HUAI RIVER

• Gaoyou (23)
Xuyi (25) •   • Yangzhou (24)

Nanjing

Wuhan
• Yichang   Shanghai •

Hangzhou

YANGTZI RIVER

Nanchang (26) •

Changsha (5, 6, 7, 8)

Fuzhou

N A N L I N G   M O U N T I A N S

Guangzhou (9)

PEARL RIVER

0   KILOMETRES   400

Occupants of tombs

1 Liu Sheng, King of Zhong Shan, and his consort
2 King of Lü
3 Kings of Chu
4 Kings of Liang
5 Queen of Changsha
6 King of Changsha
7 King of Changsha
8 Wu Zhu, King of Changsha
9 Zhao Mo (Hu), King of Nanyue
10 Queen of Guang Yang
11 Liu Jian, King of Guang Yang, and his consort
12 Liu Xiu, King of Zhong Shan
13 Zhang Er, King of Zhao
14 Liu Pi Jiang, King of He Jian, and his consort
15 Liu Shun, King of Chang Shan
16 King of Qi
17 Liu Kuan, King of Ji Bei
18 Liu Pi Guang, King of Ji Nan
19 Queen of Zi Chuan
20 Kings of Lu
21 Liu Bo, King of Chang Yi
22 King of Si Shui
23 Liu Xu, King of Guang Ling, and his consort
24 Liu Shou, King of Guang Ling, and his consort
25 Liu Fei, King of Jiang Du
26 Liu He, Marquis of Haihun

Fig 109 Royal tombs of the Western Han Dynasty

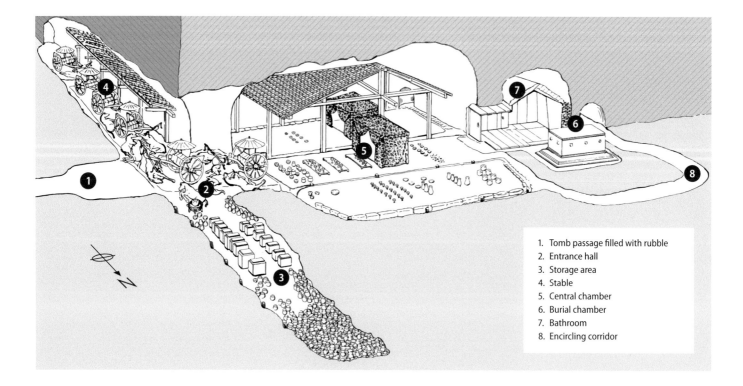

1. Tomb passage filled with rubble
2. Entrance hall
3. Storage area
4. Stable
5. Central chamber
6. Burial chamber
7. Bathroom
8. Encircling corridor

Fig 110 Liu Sheng's tomb
(after Mancheng Han mu, Beijing:
Wenwu chubanshe, 1980)

stone figures, two male and two female, guarded the entrance and the door to the bathroom. A lacquer tray had been placed in the centre of the chamber with wine and serving vessels and the remains of a slaughtered pig. Iron armour was found, as were Liu Sheng's personal weapons which were originally placed in the coffins installed on a low platform on the right side of this chamber. The bathroom on the left side was equipped with large containers, lamps and a gold inlaid incense burner. This must have functioned as a private apartment for the deceased as most of the personal articles, including the jade suit, were found here and the construction materials were more durable than the other chambers.

The rest of the royal tombs in the eastern kingdoms all have similar structures although they vary in scale, depending on the economic situation during their construction. One worthy of note, given it was found intact and is a rare example of a Han tomb from a non-Liu family, is that of the second King of Nanyue, Zhao Mo. This spectacular tomb is also almost contemporary with the tomb of Emperor Jing in Xi'an and that of the King of Zhongshan discussed earlier. It was found on the hill of Xianggang, west of Yuexiu Park in Guangzhou, and excavated in 1983. Seals found among the funerary offerings identified the tomb occupant as Zhao Mo, grandson of the founder of the Nanyue kingdom, Zhao Tuo, and successor to the throne after his grandfather's 67-year reign (r 203-137 BC). Like his grandfather, he adopted the Han imperial title and referred to himself as Wendi (Emperor Wen) despite the existence of a Han emperor in the north. Although there are very few written records about the Nanyue kingdom, it is clear that in many ways it copied systems from the Han court. This can be seen in the tomb structure, the bureaucratic system apparent in its inscriptions, the grave goods and the remains of an excavated palace building.

The tomb of Zhao Mo was dug into the earth and then tunnelled into the rock of the hill to create six chambers for different functions. Utensils for daily use were found in the western chamber which functioned as a storage room; musical instruments and banquet utensils were found in the eastern chamber which were the living quarters; animal bones and the remains of seven human attendants were found in what was the kitchen in the western side chamber (one of the attendants was identified as a leading chef by the seal found on her body); four concubines with luxurious jade burial pendants were found in the eastern side chamber; additional luxurious personal objects, including pendants and seals were found in the main chamber which functioned as the Nanyue King's bedroom; and finally, cooking utensils and liquid containers were stacked behind the King's bedroom in a rear storage room. The tomb structure, its rooms and its contents bear a strong similarity to the tombs of members of the Han imperial Liu family.[137]

We know that the practice of creating tombs to mimic the homes of the living started in the Warring States Period, particularly in the Qin and Chu regions, and that the concept matured and became widespread after the unification of China. Although the Han emperors' tombs have not been

Fig 111 Jade suit
Western Han Dynasty (2nd century BC)
Jade, 173 x 44 cm (at the shoulders)
Museum of the King of Nanyue

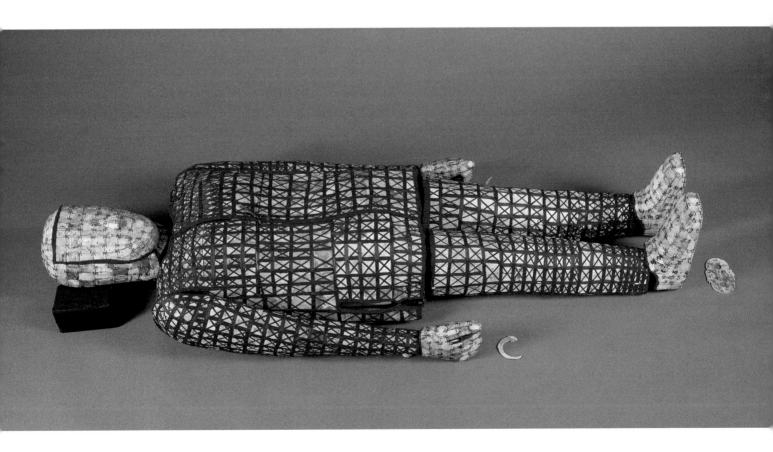

opened yet, they were almost certainly designed as underground palaces and their occupants were probably buried with a jade suit, like the royal family members in the east.

Evidence from bamboo slips found in tomb M1 at Fangmatan, Gansu, reveals that by the end of the fourth century BC, the afterlife had its bureaucratic structures just as the living world did, and dealings with the afterlife system conformed to the norms of Warring States bureaucracies.[138] This belief even extended to the formal correspondence addressed to the underground offices, informing the underworld authorities of the date of arrival of the newly deceased. This belief endured into the Han Dynasty,[139] and possibly until the end of the Chinese Empire itself in 1911.

PREPARING FOR
THE AFTERLIFE

If we consider the size of the mausoleums and the large quantities of burial items in the tombs discussed here, it becomes apparent that it would have been a considerable feat to create an underground city for the Emperor's afterlife in the short period between their accession and their death. However, this was not the end of the process and even once the tomb was closed there was still work to do; the tomb passage was sealed, trees were planted on the tomb mound as a defence against tomb robbers, family shrines were built on the tomb so that descendants could offer food and drink, and sometimes a village was created nearby and people moved in to guard the tomb. The whole process involved a large workforce and a high degree of teamwork, and was possibly organised by ritual specialists known as Tomb Officers (*mu daifu*), who were mentioned in the *Zhou li*.[140]

Later texts recorded that the Han emperor started building his mausoleum when he succeeded to the throne, allocating at least one third of the national tax income to be spent on the project.[141] A blueprint of the tomb layout would have been presented to the Emperor for approval, then tomb construction and the preparation of burial items were carefully organised in order to finish the task on time. A bronze plate, engraved with the complete design for the funerary park of King Cuo of the Zhongshan kingdom and his royal family members, dating to the Warring States Period was excavated during an archaeological dig between 1974-8. The inscriptions on this plan (*zhaoyu tu*) record that another copy of the same plan was stored in the palace.[142] It is very likely

Fig 112 Large disc, possibly a
coffin decoration
Han Dynasty (c 2nd century BC)
Jade, 43.2 cm diameter
Shaanxi Institute of Archaeology

that blueprints of royal tombs existed in various materials and were
widespread long before the unification of China.

Labourers and artisans involved in the tomb construction must have
lived near to the mausoleum for easy transportation to the site, and their
food and accommodation would have been provided. The construction
process involved digging the tomb into a rocky mountain side (in the case
of Han royal tombs in eastern China), hollowing out the various chambers
within, disposing of the excavated waste, and then smoothing and
polishing the walls of the tomb passages and chambers. Builders worked
on national projects as a way of paying their taxes,[143] but criminals were
also among the workforce. Therefore, the construction project needed to
be guarded by soldiers and supervised by the tomb planners to ensure
the work remained on schedule.

From the archaeological finds discovered it is possible to identify
three main types of burial goods: objects used by the owner during
their lifetime, such as pendants, seals and drinking and eating utensils;
funeral tributes given by other kingdoms or tribes;[144] and objects made

specifically for the funeral such as the jade suit, orifice plugs, discs, the coffin and pottery models of officials, warriors, servants and entertainers. The production of this third group of objects needed to begin soon after the emperor or king succeeded to the throne, especially the jade suit of the Han Dynasty and the stone armour from the First Emperor's burial pit as both took so long to make.

In order to finish these tasks in time for the burial, many items needed to be prepared on a production line in several workshops at once. The stone armour production, for example, would have involved a blueprint being sent to the workshop, and from this the number of stone plaques required could have been calculated. Work would have been divided amongst a team whose roles would have included cutting the stone plaques, making them into the desired shapes, drilling the holes, filing, grinding and polishing the surfaces, preparing the copper strips and lacing the plaques together.

The most difficult task would have been to cut the plaques to the required thickness of 0.5cm. In order to make the best use of material, the maximum thickness of the plaques would be 1cm. If the plaques were too thick then more labour would be needed to shape them. The drilling of between eight and twelve small attachment holes within each 7 x 6 cm plaque also presented a challenge. The holes had to be small and drilled precisely from both sides so as to meet in the middle, otherwise the plaques would break during drilling.

Analysis of the metal strips that held the plaques together indicates that the strips were hammered after annealing (heating then shaping), and that they were made from copper with small amounts of lead, tin, zinc and iron. In the process of armour restoration, archaeologists have estimated that it took 341-441 working hours to make one set of armour composed of 600 plaques. Modern technology reduces that to 146 working hours. The same labourious process also applied to the jade suits of the later Han Dynasty.

The funeral organisers, *mu dai fu*, played a crucial role in managing and controlling the various teams and workshops as they prepared for the Emperor's afterlife. However, they are hardly mentioned in any text records. In the *Han shu* there is a brief mention that the *Dong Yuan* office (The Eastern Park) worked under an official called the *Shao Fu*,[145] and that its craftsmen were responsible for making coffins and other goods for

Fig 114 Armour fragment showing individual plaques
Qin Dynasty (221-206 BC)
Limestone, 35 x 30 cm
Shaanxi Institute of Archaeology

sacrificial and mourning use. Considering the large number of members of the imperial family and aristocrats recorded in the texts, it would seem impossible for one imperial workshop to have had the capacity to produce such a large quantity of goods. Therefore, it seems highly likely that each kingdom in the Han Empire would have had their own workshop preparing these funeral goods for their authority figures.

THE ROLE OF JADE IN THE AFTERLIFE

A comparison of major tombs dating from the late Spring and Autumn Period to the Han Dynasty reveals a great increase in the use of jade between the third and second centuries BC. Some of these types of jade had come into use long before the political unifications of the Qin and Han, however, the Han Period saw a great expansion in all types of jade items.[146] The unification of China under the Qin and Han also brought together many regional burial practices, and as a result new varieties of jade object, such as the jade suit, vessels and weapons, may have developed. These jades can be classified into three main categories according to the locations in which they were found in tombs: those that represented the deceased's status in the afterlife, ie seals and pendants; jade vessels designed to prolong life; and protective jades, ie suits, discs, orifice plugs and weapons which made up the majority. To explain this increase in the use of jade, we need to examine both the tomb structures and recent archaeological finds, particularly bamboo slips.

Protection in the afterlife, both physical and spiritual, was of great concern to the designers of royal tombs. The intact tomb of Liu Sheng at Mancheng is dug into a mountainside, and the entrance has two walls of compacted earth, between which a cast iron door was inserted. In Nanyue Wang's case, a stone gate with a self-locking device in the floor was installed. Sixteen huge rectangular stones were used to block the tomb passage of Shizishan, Xuzhou which belonged to a king of the Chu kingdom, and large quantities of weapons were commonly found in Han tombs, indicating the tomb owner's desire for protection in the afterlife. These well-designed defence systems are reminiscent of the First Qin Emperor's mausoleum at Lishan:

> "Replicas of palaces, scenic towers, and the hundred officials, as well as rare utensils and wonderful objects, were brought to fill up the tomb. Craftsmen were ordered to set up crossbows and arrows, rigged so they would immediately shoot down anyone attempting to break in".[147]

In general, the number and variety of weapons increased as the intruder approached the rear tomb chamber. For example, three bronze swords, a dagger, a knife, a crossbow, arrowheads, four iron swords, two halberds, a spear, a bow and armour were found in the rear chamber of Liu Sheng's tomb, and the entrance was blocked with a thick stone with a self-locking device. Liu Sheng himself was buried inside a jade suit and carried two iron swords and a knife.

Bronze crossbows and arrowheads were commonly seen in the tomb passage, the stable, the ceremonial chamber and in the rear chamber of royal tombs. Bamboo slips excavated from a burial at Shuihudi, Hubei (dated to 217 BC),[148] explain their significance in the Shuihudi demonography, and show the demonifugal bow and arrow (a bow and arrow for destroying demons) being used to counter spectral attacks.[149] These different levels of protection may reflect the fear of the tomb owner, and it can be argued that the tomb was protected as much against spirits as against mortal attackers.

The *Jie* (Spellbinding) section of 'daybooks' from the Shuihudi instructs people on how to protect themselves from demons. Similar records are also seen in the *Wushier bing fang* (Recipes for Fifty-Two Ailments) from Mawangdui of the Han Dynasty.[150] These bamboo slips reveal that during this period people in the south of China, and probably elsewhere, believed that demonic intrusion was a significant cause of illness. Special recipes including magical, exorcising mixtures and therapeutic treatments were taken to cure disease.[151] It is also quite possible that rather than seeing decomposition as a natural process, the Han people thought that the body decomposed due to attack by evil spirits. A ritual was recorded in the *Zhou li* in which the *Fangxiangshi* (a shaman) enters the tomb wearing an animal skin and mask, and uses a spear to attack the *fangliang* demons.[152] This ritual was performed before the burial of the dead as it was imperative to purify the grave and to protect the corpse from attack by demons.[153]

As well as these rituals, a range of curses, incantations and talismans were also employed in the lower strata of Han society, particularly from the end of the first century AD onwards.[154] They were used in tombs to ensure a safe afterlife for the deceased. Jades were always found close to the body, as in the case of the intact tomb of Liu Sheng where jade plugs were inserted into the nine orifices before the body was covered with jade discs and then encased in a jade suit. The whole body was completely covered with several layers of stone, indicating the power and importance of jade in the protection of the body. Contemporary texts and bamboo slips confirm that the ancient Chinese people regarded jade and other stones as providing defence against demons and spirits, therefore jades were employed in several forms in order to ward off demons and protect the tomb occupant from attack in the afterlife.[155]

Fig 115 Water clock
Han Dynasty (c 2nd century BC)
Bronze, 32.3 x 11.3 cm
Maoling Museum

HAN TECHNOLOGY

Han China was a period of economic prosperity, characterised by significant advances in science, technology, mathematics, astronomy and literature. It is thought to have been the most technically advanced empire in the world at the time. Seismographic instruments were invented to predict earthquakes, irrigation and water conservation technologies were introduced to improve agriculture, a water clock was created to calculate the time, and paper came into circulation. Medicine was also very advanced in this period: Hua Tuo (c 140-208) was the first person in China to use anaesthesia during surgery. He was also known as a master of acupuncture, herbal medicine and medical *Daoyin* exercises which involve imitating the movements of the tiger, ape, deer, bear and crane. Drawings of *Daoyin* exercises[156] and a lacquer acupuncture figure[157] have been found in Western Han tombs, dating to almost a century before Hua Tuo, and are still practised today.

CONTACT WITH THE OUTSIDE WORLD

From the very earliest written records on the oracle bones of the Shang (c 1250-1045 BC), we know that the people in the region of the Yellow River basin, who we now call the Chinese, had constantly engaged in warfare and trade with their northern neighbours.[158] Horses, chariots and weapons, as well as belt hooks and plaques for ornament, were all traded.[159] Twenty-five earthenware moulds and bronze casting tools for belt plaques bearing Steppe motifs were found in a late Warring States Qin tomb (c 350-221 BC) during the construction of the modern-day Lebaishi Company, Xi'an. The tomb occupant was likely to have been the craftsman or a related official.[160] This suggests that the belt plaques, with their exotic patterns, were made in China for the foreign market in the Steppes and also to satisfy the domestic needs of Chinese rulers.

The Han Period saw increased contact between China and the outside world, the evidence for which is found in text records and archaeological finds. With the introduction of Buddhism to China during the Eastern Han Period, foreign travellers such as monks from Parthia (Iran) and India journeyed to China and translated the Buddhist sutra into Chinese. The Han Empire also received diplomatic gifts from other countries.

Fig 116 Mould for belt plaque with horse motif
Qin Dynasty (221-206 BC)
Ceramic, 9.4 x 7 cm
Shaanxi Institute of Archaeology

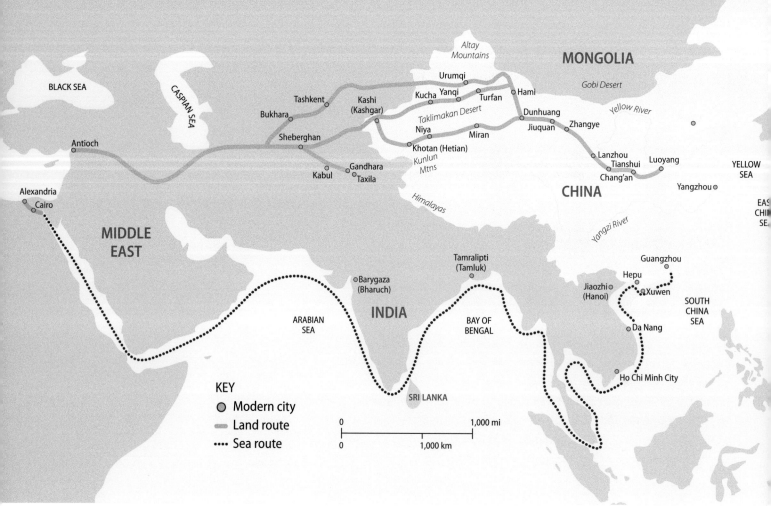

The nomadic Steppe people, the Xiongnu, had been invading Chinese territory since the Warring States Period and continued their raids on the Han borders. The Han Empire was forced to make substantial gifts to the Xiongnu and even married off Han princesses to make peace with their neighbours. It was not until the Han Emperor Wu (r 141-87) launched several successful military campaigns against them that the Xiongnu finally accepted vassal status in the Han Empire. This expanded the Han's territory into central Asia, helping to establish the vast trade network of Silk Routes that linked Xi'an to the Mediterranean coast, and creating new opportunities for merchants in the process. They traded silk, tea, porcelain, lacquerware, salt and spices in exchange for gold, silver, jade, ivory, glass and exotic goods.

The Han military expansion during the reign of Emperor Wu also extended Chinese territory to Korea in the east, north Vietnam in the south and the Hexi corridor in the west. This increased trade and the economic prosperity of the Empire, and led to cultural exchanges between several peoples. As a result Chinese silks appeared in the markets of the Roman Empire and Persian coins, exotic materials and new

Fig 117 The road and maritime silk routes, 3rd century BC - 3rd century AD

Fig 118 Stone weight in the form of a lion
Western Han Dynasty (2nd century BC)
Stone, 23.5 x 13 x 14.5 cm
Xuzhou Museum

Fig 119 Discs with Greek script, decorated with dragon motif, likely used as coins
Han Dynasty (206 BC-AD 220)
Lead, 5.5 x 1 cm
Changwu County Museum

Fig 120 Disc-shaped ingots
Han Dynasty (202 BC-AD 220)
Gold
Shaanxi History Museum

designs arrived in China, making their way into high-ranking individuals' tombs. Roman glassware and coins have also been found in China, and Roman medallions from the reign of Antoninus Pius and his adopted son, Marcus Aurelius, have been found in Vietnam.

From the archaeological finds discovered we can see that almost all of the royal Liu family members possessed exotic objects that were either made in China using Steppe designs or imported from that region. Other objects they possessed are cultural hybrids. For example, incense burners in the tombs of Liu Sheng and his consort at Mancheng, Hebei are shaped like peaked mountains and have features of the Steppe, Iran and China.[161] In the tomb of Chu King (c 175-154 BC) at Shizishan, Xuzhou an exquisite jade suit has been found. It came from Khotan, Xinjiang, which was beyond the Chinese border at the time, while a marble lion mattress weight in the form of a seated lion on a platform with a loop on the neck and a seashell collar, also indicates links with central Asia.[162]

The tomb of the King of Jiangdu, Liu Fei (r 169-129 BC), discovered at Xuyi, Jiangsu in 2010, contained a silver box with tear-shaped lobes in a Persian style, along with a small set of bronze sculptures of a rhinoceros

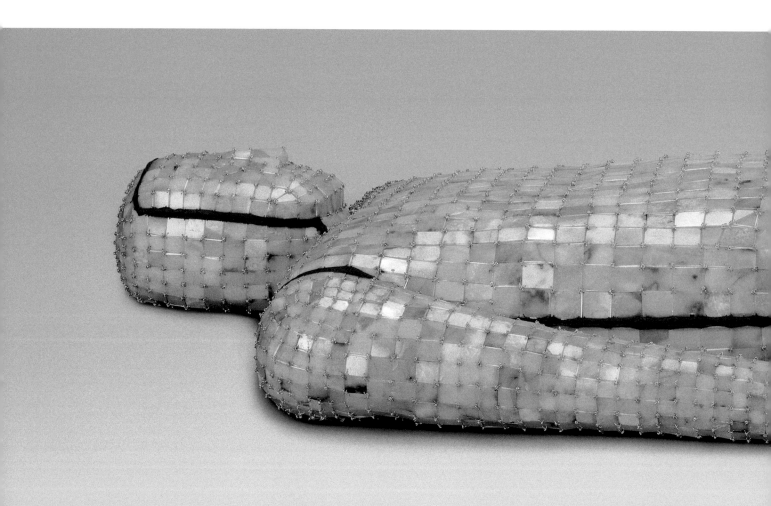

and groom. Both the groom and animal have non-Chinese features.[163] Even if these exotic designs were made in China for the imperial Liu family members, the originals on which they were based came from the Steppes or even further west. The artists must have seen the original objects in order to copy the designs.

As well as the overland silk routes, maritime silk routes were also very busy during the Han Period. The accidentally discovered Han tomb in Guangzhou, which belonged to the King of Nanyue (see pages 122-123), contained a large number of exotic objects. These included 32 gold buttons with floral designs and inlaid gems with a possible link to Mesopotamia; rare gold ornaments in the shape of an apricot leaf that are commonly found in the tombs of Liu royal family members; a Persian-style silver box with tear-shaped lobes; a jade rhyton (conical cup) with strong central Asian influences; bronze containers, *titong,* that may have links with northern Vietnam, and elephant tusks that have been identified as originating in Africa.[164] Although some of the luxurious and exotic objects found in the tomb of the King of Nanyue might have arrived through trade and gift exchanges, the majority are likely to have arrived via the maritime silk routes. Further evidence includes octagonal columns found in the palace of the King of Nanyue, Guangzhou. The director of Nanyue Palace Museum, Hong Quan, suggests that the columns might

Fig 121 Rhinoceros and groom
Western Han Dynasty (2nd century BC)
Gilt bronze, 19.8 x 8.4 x 9.8 cm (rhinoceros)
Nanjing Museum

Fig 122 Jade suit
Western Han Dynasty (2nd century BC)
Jade, 175 x 68 cm
Xuzhou Museum

have been shipped by sea from Egypt, Rome or Persia via India.[165] As Nanyue claimed to be an independent kingdom during various periods of its existence, and its communications with China were occasionally severed, logically its contact with the outside world must have been through the maritime silk routes.

Horses still played an important role on the battlefield, particularly when the Han were defending themselves against invasion by the nomadic Xiongnu. Horses from central Asia were imported to the Han court, and Chinese armies travelled thousands of miles west to Ferghana searching for the 'heaven horse'.[166] Foreign horse experts, possibly Mongolian, were given official titles in China when they were training,

Fig 123 Octagonal columns
2nd century BC
Volcanic rock, 20.9 x 11.6cm^2, 37.4 x 15 cm^2, 30 x 13.2 cm^2
Archaeological Site Museum of Nanyue Palace

Fig 124 Horse sculpture
Han Dynasty (c 2nd century BC)
Gilt bronze, 62 x 76 cm, 25.55 kg
Maoling Museum

Fig 125 Horse rider with Mongolian features
Han Dynasty (c 2nd century BC)
Ceramic, 54 x 8.8 cm
Han Jingdi Yangling Museum

Fig 126 Mirror with game board design
Han Dynasty (206 BC–AD 220)
Bronze, 16.8 cm diameter
Metropolitan Museum of Art, New York

managing and breeding horses for the royal family, further indicating the importance of horses to the Han.[167]

As discussed earlier, the quest for immortality was a major preoccupation of kings and nobles during the late Warring States Period and also after the unification of China. They looked to the outside world for a solution as immortals were believed to reside in the border areas of China, in the seas of the east or in the remote mountains of the

Fig 127 Winged immortal
riding a horse
Western Han Dynasty
(1st century BC)
Jade, 7.2 x 9.0 x 3.4 cm
Shaanxi Xianyang Municipal
Museum

Fig 128 A detail of fig 126
showing a winged immortal

west. For example, the First Emperor of Qin was said to have sent his
court physician, Xu Fu, and thousands of children in search of elixirs of
immortality. Also, the legend and image of the immortal goddess,
the Queen Mother of the West, were widely circulated after the silk routes
opened in the Han Period. In addition, immortals with pointed noses
and wings, which may have their origins in central Asia, appeared in Han
bronze and jade sculptures.

THE QIN AND HAN LEGACIES

Modern China retains many vestiges of both the Qin Empire and its longer-lived successor, the Han Dynasty. This is evident in the physical structures that remain but also in the beliefs and cultural practices of the Chinese people.

Much of Chinese culture can be traced back to the Han Dynasty. It was an era of peace and prosperity that allowed China to expand to become a major world power. As a result, the majority of Chinese people today are proud to be called Han *ren*, the language they speak is Han *yu*, while the characters they write with are Han *zi*. They are also proud of the trade routes that were created during the Han Empire and which served to link east and west. It can truly be called the Golden Age of Ancient China.

Fig 129 Figure being excavated

The Han love of jade also endures. The use of jade reached a peak during this period of Chinese history – it was more valuable than gold - and although it declined after the collapse of the Han Dynasty, jade's magical power had become deeply rooted within the Chinese mind. This explains an obsession with the stone that has lasted until the present day.

Similarly, like both the Qin and the Han, most Chinese people still believe in the afterlife. In preparation for funerals they purchase paper figures and furniture for their deceased family members, and burn them after the funeral ceremony. In addition, there is an obsession with taking medicine, as it is believed that medicines can cure diseases and prolong life, even to the point of achieving immortality.

The Qin influence is probably best evidenced by the physical structures that remain. The Great Wall of China, the road network, the Lingqu Canal and of course the First Emperor's tomb are all prominent relics of the Qin's extreme ambition and power. The Emperor may not have succeeded in his quest for physical immortality but his fame lives on, and there is little doubt that it will grow in coming years. Archaeologists plan to conduct an extensive survey of Qin Shi Huang's burial site, using modern geophysical survey techniques and ground penetrating radar to collect data. This will be combined with satellite images and mapping software to create 3D and 4D models of the site, both above and below ground. Technologies will be able to produce a much more comprehensive record and a more accurate visualisation of the entire complex, allowing archaeologists to investigate the Emperor's mausoleum without opening up his tomb. No doubt there are many more wonders to be discovered and secrets to be revealed.

NOTES

CHAPTER 1

1. Hongshan sites are widespread, ranging from Inner Mongolia to Liaoning province. Tombs at Hutougou see *Wenwu* 1984.6, pp.1-5; tombs from Niuheliang see *Wenwu* 1986.8, pp.1-17, 18-24, also *Wenwu* 1997.8, pp.4-14, 15-19
2. See Rawson 1995, p.33; Rawson 1998a, p.33; also Beijing & Hong Kong 1989
3. The reuse of earlier jades in the Shang period has been discussed by Hayashi and Rawson. See Hayashi 1991, pp.515-576; Rawson 1997, pp.171-188
4. Keightley 1999, pp.232-291
5. Rawson 1990, pp.17-61
6. While most scholars have argued that the sophistication of Shang bronzes and jades was copied by people on the periphery, Rawson suggests this exchange also took place in the other direction. She further points out that the Shang may have traded, seized and copied both bronzes and jades from their neighbours. See Rawson 1995, p.40
7. Bagley 1980, p.194
8. Thote 2013, p.38
9. Bagley 1980, pp.194-199
10. Rawson 1990, p.32
11. Bagley 1980, p.196
12. Shaughnessy 1999, p.293
13. Rawson 1990, pp.37-38
14. Bagley 1980, p.241

CHAPTER 2

15. Hsu 1999, pp.545-586
16. Lewis 1999, p.620
17. Pines 2013, pp.27-35
18. Rawson 1998b, p.126
19. Wu 1999, pp.651-744
20. Wu 1999, p.726; Thorp 1981-82, p.76. Examples from Baoshan tomb M2 (c 316 BC), see Beijing 1991a, pp.265-277; Beijing 1991b, pp.13-14
21. Lin 2012d, pp.82-89
22. *Shjji*, p.685; Pines 2013, p.28
23. Shaughnessy 2013, pp.23-25
24. *Guangming Daily News* 1986.5.2; 1986.5.3; 1986.5.4; 1986.5.24; 1986.6.8 and *Antiquary* 1986.9, pp.19-26; Thote 2013, pp.41-42
25. *Wenwu* 1993.10, pp.1-14, 15-19; *Kaogu yu wenwu* 1993.3, pp.35-39; Thote 2013, p.42
26. Pines 2013, pp.28-29
27. Yates 2007, pp.31-35
28. Pines 2013, p.30
29. Pines 2013, pp.106-115
30. Pines 2013, pp.28-35

CHAPTER 3

31. *Shiji 6*, Dawson translation, 2009, pp.3-5
32. *Shiji 6*, p. 2542
33. Pines et al. 2014, pp.1-4
34. Lindersay and Guo 1999, p.4
35. Lin 1991, p. 9
36. Pines 2013, pp.105-116
37. Loewe 2007, pp.59-79
38. Liu 2012, pp.136-138
39. Yunmeng 1981; Shuihudi 2001
40. Loewe 2007, pp.59-79
41. Hulsewé 1985, pp.145-146
42. Liu 2012, pp.140-141
43. Beijing 2012
44. Zhang Zaiming et al. 2006; The survey of the Qin Straight Road was listed in "China's top 10 archaeological discoveries of 2009" by the State Administration of Cultural Heritage.
45. Shelach 2014, pp.113-138
46. Needham 1971, pp.299-306
47. Pines 2013, pp.27-37
48. Huo 1998, pp.91-99
49. Lindersay and Guo 1999, pp.4-5
50. Di Cosmo 2002, pp.161-252
51. Loewe 2013, pp.237-248
52. Liu 2012, pp.138-141
53. Loewe 2007, pp. 59-79
54. Ibid
55. Wang 2007, pp. 80-82
56. Shelach 2014, pp.113-138
57. Rawson 2007, pp.114-145
58. Kinoshita 2007, pp.83-93

59. Liu 2012, pp.138-141
60. Kern 2007, pp.105-113
61. Ibid
62. Loewe 2007, pp.59-79

Chapter 4

63. Rawson 2007, pp.114-145
64. Beijing 1998a
65. Beijing 2000, pp.1-32
66. Lindersay and Guo 1999, pp.4-6
67. Rawson 2007, pp.114-145
68. Yuan 2002, pp.15-20
69. Duan 2011, pp.211-228
70. Kern 2007, pp.105-113
71. Cao and Zhang 2011, pp.49-78
72. Li et al. 2011, pp.492-501
73. Yuan 2002, pp.15-16
74. Duan 2011, pp.31-68
75. Yuan et al. 2005
76. Rawson 2007, pp.114-145
77. Zhang 2013, p.112
78. Yuan 1990, 2014, pp.383-401
79. Li Xiuzhen et al, 2016, pp.169-183
80. Yuan 2002, p.327
81. Beijing 2007, pp.194-206
82. Xu et al. 2008, pp.1-7
83. Ibid
84. Yuan 2002, pp.124-135
85. Li 2007, pp.429-443
86. Quinn et al. 2017, pp.966-979
87. Beijing 2007, pp.194-206
88. Zhang and Cao 2014, pp.6-9
89. Rawson 2007, pp.114-145
90. *Shiji* 6, p.265
91. Selbitschka 2013, pp.144-154
92. Yuan 2002, p.55
93. Selbitschka 2013, pp.144-154
94. Beijing 2007, pp.194-206
95. Beijing 1998a; Beijing 1998b
96. Beijing 2001, p.156
97. Yuan and Liu 2009, pp.82-84
98. Beijing 2006, pp.65-95
99. Yuan 2002, pp.187-198
100. Zhao 2008, p.4
101. Beijing 2000, pp.1-32
102. Yuan 2002, pp.136-144
103. Ibid
104. Rawson 2007, p.139
105. Personal communication with Dr Zhu Sihong (an archaeologist of the Emperor Qin Shi Huang's Mausoleum Site Museum) who was in charge of the excavation.
106. Lin 2007, pp.181-91
107. Beijing 2000, pp.1-32
108. Beijing 2007, pp.194-206
109. Yuan 1990; 2014, pp.380-398
110. Ledderose 2000, pp.67-73
111. Li et al. 2016, pp.169-183
112. Bevan et al. 2014, pp.249-254
113. Li et al. 2016, pp.169-183
114. Bevan et al. 2014, pp.249-254
115. Quinn et al.2017, pp.966-979

116. Lei 2004, pp.38-42
117. Blänsdorf et al. (ed) 2001, pp.340-369
118. *Shiji* 6, p.239
119. Yuan 2014, pp.380-398
120. Li 2012, pp.77-92
121. Li 2012, pp.215-219
122. Martinón-Torres et al. 2014, pp.534-562
123. Yates 2007, pp.31-37
124. Li et al. 2014, pp.126-140
125. Li et al. 2011, pp.492-501
126. Li et al. 2011, pp.492-501

Chapter 5

127. According to the *Hou Han shu*, the Vermilion Eyebrows Bandits opened up and dug out the various Han imperial tombs at Chang'an. See *Hou Han shu*, pp.483-484. Also, Xiang Yu was accused of plundering the First Qin Emperor's tomb by Liu Bang, which was recorded in *Shiji*. See *Shiji*, p.376. The plundering of Han Baling and Duling are recorded in *Jin shu*, p.1651
128. Liu & Li 1993, pp.361-370; also Liu & Ma 1990, pp.147-150
129. *Wenbo* 1999.6, pp.3-11; Beijing 2016
130. *Shiji*, pp.440-444
131. See *Shiji*, pp.2072-80; translated by Watson 1961, pp.369-380
132. See *Shiji*, p.2079; Watson, 1961, pp.379-380
133. Given concerns about rebellion, in both life and the afterlife, it does not seem possible that Zhou Yafu would have been buried with such a large terracotta army, not to mention the privileged imperial funeral article, the jade suit. Therefore, some scholars support the view that these two satellite tomb occupants are unlikely to be Zhou Bo or Zhou Yafu.
134. *Shiji*, pp.840-841; *Han shu*, p.2422
135. Wu 1997, p.151; also see Thorp 1987, p.30
136. Beijing 1980, pp.10-37; Thorp 1980, pp.51-66; Thorp 1987, pp.26-39; Wu 1997, p.151
137. More discussion on Han royal tombs in Xuzhou, see Lin 2012a, pp.49-57
138. Harper 1994, p.17
139. A famous example was found in tomb M3 at Mawangdui, Hunan. See *Wenwu* 1974.7, p.43. See also Yü 1987, p.384; see also Poo 1998, p.168
140. *Zhou li*, section 22, p.2b
141. *Jin shu*, p.1651
142. Beijing 1995, pp.104-110; Nickel 2007, p.159
143. Loewe 2007, p.74
144. It has been a long tradition in Chinese history. Lists of funeral tributes which were recorded on bamboo slips and then buried can be seen in the tomb of Marquis Yi of Zeng, dating to around 433 BC. See Beijing 1989, p.467
145. The *shao fu* is translated into lesser office by Sadao Nishijima, see Nishijima 1986, p.591

146. Jade categories in the Han period include jade vessels, sword fittings, weapons, pillows, suits, orifice plugs, coffins inlaid with jade plaques, discs, jade pendants and seals. See Lin 2012b, pp.77-83
147. Watson 1993, p.63
148. The bamboo slips were recovered from tomb M11 at Shuhudi between December 1975 and January 1976. See *Early China* 3 1977), pp.100-104; *Wenwu* 1976.5, pp.1-10; also Beijing 1977
149. Harper 1985, pp.458-498
150. Harper 1985, p.470
151. Harper 1995, pp.244-5
152. See *Zhou li*, section 31, pp.6b-7a
153. Harper 1985, pp.481-482
154. See Seidel 1987, p.708; Wu 1981, pp.56-63; *Wenwu* 1975.11, pp.75-93; *Kaogu wenwu* 1980.1, pp.44-48; *Wenwu* 1981.3, pp.53-55.
155. For more discussion on the function of jade in Han Dynasty, see Lin 2007, pp.180-191; Lin 2012b, pp.77-83.
156. Beijing 1973
157. *Wenwu* 1996, pp.10,13-29
158. Rawson 2012, p.23; Di Cosmo 1999, pp.885-966
159. Rawson 2012, pp.24-26; Hsing 2017, pp.63-73
160. Xi'an 2006, pp.120-33, 361-65
161. See Rawson 2012, pp.24-26
162. Lin 2012c, cats.35 and 87
163. Sun 2017, cat.92
164. Lin 2012c, cats.122, 158, 159, 167
165. Quan 2012, p.39
166. *Shiji*, p.3170; Watson 1961, p.240
167. Evidence can be seen on Mongolian pottery horse riders found in both Han Yangling in Xian, Shaanxi Province and Shizishan in Xuzhou, Jiangsu Province in Lin 2012c, cat.1

BIBLIOGRAPHY

Bagley 1980
Robert W Bagley, "The Rise of the Western Zhou Dynasty", *The Great Bronze Age of China*, New York: The Metropolitan Museum of Art 1980, pp.193-213

Beijing 1936
Zhou li周禮, *Sibu beiyao*, repr. Beijing: Zhonghua shuju, 1936

Beijing 1959
Shiji 史記 by Sima Qian (司馬遷 c 145-86 BC), Beijing:Zhonghua shuju, 1959

Beijing 1960
*Hou Han shu*後漢書, by Ban Gu (班固 AD 32-92), Beijing: Zhonghua shuju, 1960

Beijing 1973
*Changsha Mawangdui yi hao Han mu*長沙馬王堆一號漢墓, 2 vols, Beijing: Wenwu Chubanshe, 1973

Beijing 1974
*Jin shu*晉書, comp. by Fang Xuanling (房玄齡 578-648), Beijing: Zhonghua shuju, 1974

Beijing 1977
*Shuihudi Qinmu zhujian*睡虎地秦墓竹簡, Beijing: Wenwu chubanshe, 1977

Beijing 1980
*Mancheng Han mu fajue baogao*滿城漢墓發掘報告, 2 vols, Beijing: Wenwu Chubanshe, 1980

Beijing 1981
Yunmeng Shuihudi Qinmu Bianxiezu雲夢睡虎地秦墓編寫組, *Yunmeng Shuihudi Qin mu*雲夢睡虎地秦墓, Beijing: Wenwu chubanshe, 1981

Beijing 1989
*Zeng Hou Yi mu*曾侯乙墓, Beijing: Wenwu chubanshe, 1989

Beijing 1991a
*Baoshan Chumu*包山楚墓, 2 vols, Beijing: Wenwu Chubanshe, 1991

Beijing 1991b
*Baoshan Chujian*包山楚簡, Beijing: Wenwu chubanshe, 1991

Beijing 1995
*Cuo mu - Zhanguo Zhongshanguo guwang zhi mu*뿔墓戰國中山國王之墓, Beijing: Wenwu chubanshe, 1995

Beijing 1998a
Museum of Qin Shihuang's Terracotta Army and Shaanxi Institute of Archaeology秦始皇兵马俑博物馆和陕西省考古所, *Qin Shihuang ling tongchema fajue baogao*秦始皇陵铜车马发掘报告, Beijing: Kexue chubanshe, 1998

Beijing 1998b
Museum of Qin Shihuang's Terracotta Army 秦始皇兵马俑博物馆, *Qin Shihuang ling tongchema xiufu baogao*秦始皇陵铜车马修复报告, Beijing: Kexue chubanshe, 1998

Beijing 2000
Shaanxi Institute of Archaeology and Museum of Qin Terracotta Army陝西省考古所和秦兵馬俑博物館. *Qin Shihuang lingyuan kaogu baogao 1999*秦始皇陵園考古報告1999, Beijing: Wenwu chubanshe, 2000

Beijing 2001
Shuihudi Qinmu zhujian zhengli xiaozhu睡虎地秦墓竹简整理小组, *Shuihudi Qin mu zhujian* 睡虎地秦墓竹简, Beijing: Wenwu chubanshe, 2001

Beijing 2006
Shaanxi Institute of Archaeology and Museum of Qin Terracotta Army陝西省考古所和秦兵馬俑博物館, *Qinshihuangdi lingyuan kaogu baogao 2000*秦始皇帝陵園考古報告2000, Beijing: Wenwu chubanshe, 2006

Beijing 2007
Shaanxi Institute of Archaeology and Museum of Qin Terracotta Army陝西省考古所和秦兵馬俑博物館, *Qinshihuangdi lingyuan kaogu baogao 2001-2003*秦始皇帝陵園考古報告2001-2003, Beijing: Wenwu chubanshe, 2007

Beijing 2012
Hunan Provincial Institute of Archaeology湖南省考古所, *Liye qinjian - yi* 裏耶秦簡 - 壹, Beijing: Wenwu chubanshe, 2012

Beijing 2016
*Han Yangling*漢陽陵, Beijing: Wenwu chubanshe, 2016

Beijing & Hong Kong 1989
*Liangzhu Wenhua Yuqi*良渚文化玉器, Beijing: Wenwu chubanshe and Hong Kong: The Woods Publishing Company, 1989

Bevan 2014
Andrew Bevan, Xiuzhen Li, Marcos Martinón-Torres, Susan Green, Yin Xia, Kun Zhao, Zen Zhao, Shengtao Ma, Wei Cao and Thilo Rehren, "Computer vision, archaeological classification and China's Terracotta Warriors", *Journal of Archaeological Science*, 2014, 49 (1), pp.249-254

Blänsdorf 2001
Catharina Blänsdorf, Erwin Emmerling, and Michael Petzet (ed), *The Terracotta Army of the First Chinese Emperor Qin Shihuang*, München: Monuments and Sites, 2001

Cao and Zhang 2011
Cao Wei and Zhang Weixing 曹瑋和張衛星, "Qinshihuangdi lingyuan kaoguo de lishi xianzhuang yu yanjiu silu 秦始皇帝陵考古的歷史、現狀和研究思路", *Qinshihuangdi ling bowuyuan yuankan*秦始皇帝陵博物院院刊 vol 1, 2011, pp.49-78

Di Cosmo 1999
Nicola Di Cosmo, "The Northern Frontier in Pre-Imperial China", *The Cambridge History of Ancient China - from the Origins of Civilization to 221 BC* (ed Loewe and Shaughnessy), Cambridge: Cambridge University Press, 1999, pp.885-966

Di Cosmo 2002
Nicola Di Cosmo, *Ancient China and its enemies: The rise of Nomadic power in East Asian history*, Cambridge: Cambridge University Press, 2002

Dawson 2009
Raymond Dawson (translates), "*Sima Qian: The First Emperor, selection from Shiji, Historical Records*", Oxford: Oxford University Press, 2009

Duan 2011
Duan Qingbo 段清波, *Qinshihuangdi lingyuan kaogu yanjiu* 秦始皇帝陵園考古研究, Beijing: Beijing daxue chubanshe, 2011

Harper 1985
Donald Harper, "A Chinese Demonography of the Third Century BC", *Harvard Journal of Asiatic Studies*, 1985(45), 2, pp.458-498

Harper 1994
Donald Harper, "Resurrection in Warring States Popular Religion", *Taoist Resources*, 1994, vol 5, no 2, pp.13-28

Harper 1995
Donald Harper, "The Bellows Analogy in Laozi V And Warring States Macrobiotic Hygiene", *Early China*, 1995, pp.381-391

Hayashi 1991
Minao Hayashi, "Inkyo Fuko-bo-shutsudo no gyokki jakkan ni taisuru chushaku", *Tohogakuho*, vol 58, republished in *Chūgoku kogyoku no kenkyū*中國古玉の研究, Tokyo: Yoshikawa Kobunkan, 1991, pp.515-576

Hsing 2017
I-Tien Hsing, "Qin-Han China and the Outside World', *Age of Empires - Art of the Qin and Han Dynasties*, New York: The Metropolitan Museum of Art, 2017, pp.63-73

Hsu 1999
Cho-Yun Hsu, "The Spring and Autumn Period", *The Cambridge History of Ancient China - from the Origins of Civilization to 221 BC* (ed Loewe and Shaughnessy), Cambridge: Cambridge University Press, 1999, pp.545-586

Huang 1998
Huang Xuanpei黄宣佩, "Qijia wenhua yu liqi 齊家文化玉禮器", *East Asian Jade: Symbol of Excellence*, HK: The Chinese University of Hong Kong 1998 vol 1, pp.184-191

Hulsewé 1985
AFP Hulsewé, *Remnants of Ch'in Law: An Annotated Translation of the Ch'in Legal and Administrative Rules of the 3rd Century BC Discovered in Yun-meng Prefecture, Hupei Province in 1975*, Leiden: Brill Academic Publishers, 1985

Huo 1998
Huo Yinzhang霍印章, *Zhongguo junshi tongshi, vol 4: Qin dai junshi shi*中国军事通史第四卷：秦代军事史, Beijing: Junshi kexue chubanshe, 1998

Keightley 1999
David N Keightley, "The Shang: China's First Historical Dynasty", *The Cambridge History of Ancient China - from the Origins of Civilization to 221 BC* (ed Loewe and Shaughnessy), Cambridge: Cambridge University Press, 1999, pp.232-291

Kern 2007
Martin Kern, "Imperia tours and mountain inscriptions", *The First Emperor China's Terracotta Army* (ed Jane Portal), London: The British Museum Press, 2007, pp.104-113

Kinoshita 2007
Hiromi Kinoshita, "Qin Palaces and Architecture", *The First Emperor China's Terracotta Army* (ed Jane Portal), London: The British Museum Press, 2007, pp.83-93

Ledderose 2000
Lather Ledderose, *Ten thousand things: module and mass production in Chinese art*, Princeton: Princeton University Press, 2000

Lei 2004
Lei Yong, Guo Baofa, and Yuan Sixun, "Neutron activation analysis for the provenance study on Terracotta Army of Qin Shihuang", *Nuclear Techniques*, 2004, vol 27, pp.38-42

Lewis 1999
Mark Edward Lewis, "Warring States Political History", *The Cambridge History of Ancient China—from the Origins of Civilization to 221 BC* (ed Loewe and Shaughnessy), Cambridge: Cambridge University Press, 1999, pp.587-650

Li 2007
Xiuzhen Li 李秀珍,"Cong Qinshihuang lingqu taoyao de fenbu kan lingqu taozhipin deshaozhi 從秦始皇陵區陶窑的分佈看陵區陶製品的燒製", *Research on Qin Terracotta Warriors and Qin Culture*秦俑秦文化研究, vol 14, Xian: Shaanxi chubanshe, 2007, pp.429-443

Li 2012
Xiuzhen Li, *Standardisation, Labour Organisation and the Bronze Weapons of the Qin Terracotta Warriors*, PhD Thesis, London: University College London, 2012

Li et al. 2011
Xiuzhen Li, Marcos Martinón-Torres, Nigel Meeks, Yin Xia and Kun Zhao, "Inscriptions, filing, grinding and polishing marks on the bronze weapons from the Qin Terracotta Army in China", *Journal of Archaeological Science* 38, pp.492-501

Li et al. 2014
Xiuzhen Li, Marcos Martinón-Torres, Thilo Rehren, Wei Cao, Yin Xia, Kun Zhao, "Crossbows and imperial craft organisation: the bronze triggers of China's Terracotta Army", *Antiquity*, 2014, vol 88, pp.126-140

Li et al. 2016
Xiuzhen Li, Andrew Bevan, Marcos Martinón-Torres, Yin Xia and Kun Zhao, "Marking practice and the making of the Qin Terracotta Army", *Journal of Anthropological Archaeology*, vol 42, pp.169-183

Lin 1991
Jianming Lin 林劍鳴, *Qin Shi Gao* 秦史稿, Beijing: China Renmin University Press, 1991

Lin 2007
James CS Lin, "Armour for the Afterlife", *The First Emperor - China's Terracotta Army* (ed Jane Portal), London: The British Museum, 2007, pp.180-191

Lin 2012a
James CS Lin, "The Hierarchical Burial System of Han Tombs as Seen in Xuzhou", *The Search for Immortality—Tomb Treasure of Han China*, (ed James CS Lin), New Haven: Yale University Press, 2012, pp.49-57

Lin 2012b
James CS Lin, "Protection in the Afterlife", *The Search for Immortality - Tomb Treasures of Han China* (ed James CS Lin), New Haven: Yale University Press, 2012, pp.77-83

Lin 2012c
James CS Lin, *The Search for Immortality - Tomb Treasures of Han China* (ed James CS Lin), New Haven: Yale University Press, 2012

Lin 2012d
James CS Lin, "The Emperor's New Clothes: Dressing for the Afterlife", *Arts of Asia*, 2012, pp.82-89

Lindersay and Guo 1999
William Lindersay and Baofa Guo, *The Terracotta Army of the First Emperor of China*, Hong Kong: Odyssey Publications, 1999

Liu & Li 1993
Liu Qingzhu劉慶柱 and Li Yufang.李毓芳, "Han xuandi duling lingqing jianzhu zhidu yanjiu漢宣帝杜陵陵寝建築制度研究", *Zhongguo kaoguxue luncong*中國考古學論叢, Beijing: Kexue chubanshe 1993, pp.361-370

Liu & Ma 1990
Liu Shier劉士莪, Ma Zhenzhi馬振智 "Qin guo ling qing zhidu dui xi Han diling de yingxiang 秦國陵寝制度對西漢帝陵的影響", *Wenbo* 1990.5, pp.147-150

Liu 2012
Liu Yang, "The First Emperor: his life, achievements, and vision", *China's Terracotta Warriors – The First Emperor's Legacy* (ed Liu Yang), Minneapolis: Minneapolis Institute of Arts, 2012, pp.136-8

Loewe 2007
Michael Loewe, 'The First Emperor and the Qin Empire', *The First Emperor - China's Terracotta Army* (ed Jane Portal), London: The British Museum, 2007, pp.59-79

Loewe 2013
Michael Loewe, "The Qin and Han Empires and Their Heritage", *Qin: The Eternal Emperor and His Terracotta Warriors* (ed Maria Khayutina), Zurcher: Bernisches Historisches Museum, 2013, pp.237-247

Martinón-Torres et al. 2014
Marcos Martinón-Torres, Xiuzhen Li, Andrew Bevan, Yin Xia, Kun Zhao, Thilo Rehren, "Forty thousand arms for a single emperor: from chemical data to labor organization in the production of bronze arrows for the Terracotta Army", *Journal of Archaeological Method and Theory*, 2014, 21, pp.534–562

Needham 1971
Joseph Needham, *Science and Civilisation in China*, vol IV. 3, Cambridge, 1971.

Nickel 2007
Lukas Nickel, "The Terracotta Army", *The First Emperor—China's Terracotta Army* (ed Jane Portal), London: The British Museum, 2007, pp.159-179

Nishijima 1986
Sadao Nishijima. "The Economic and Social History of Former Han", *The Cambridge History of China*, Cambridge University Press, 1986, pp.545-607

Pines 2013
Yuri Pines, "King Zheng of Qin, the First Emperor of China", *Qin: The Eternal Emperor and His Terracotta Warriors* (ed Maria Khayutina), Zurcher: Bernisches Historisches Museum, 2013, pp. 27-35, 105-116

Pines et al. 2014
Yuri Pines, Lothar von Falkenhausen, Gideon Shelach, and Robin Yates, eds., *Birth of an empire: the State of Qin revisited*, London: University of California Press, 2014

Poo 1998
Mu-chou Poo, *In Search of Personal Welfare: A View of Ancient Chinese Religion*. Albany: State University of New York Press, 1998

Quan 2012
Quan Hong全洪, "Archaeological Discoveries Relating to the Maritime Trade of The Kingdom of Nanyue", *The Search for Immortality—Tomb Treasures of Han China* (ed James CS Lin), New Haven: Yale University Press, 2012, pp.37-41

Quinn et al. 2017
Patrick Quinn et al., "Building the Terracotta Army: Ceramic Craft Technology and Organisation of Production at Emperor Qin Shihuang's Mausoleum Complex, China", *Antiquity,* 2017, vol 93, pp.966-979

Rawson 1990
Jessica M Rawson, "Changing Values of Ancient Chinese Bronzes', *Ancient Chinese and Ordos Bronzes*, (ed Jessica M Rawson and Emma Bunker), Hong Kong: The Oriental Ceramic Society 1990, pp.17-61

Rawson 1995
Jessica M Rawson, *Chinese Jade: From the Neolithic to the Qing*, London: British Museum Press, 1995

Rawson 1997
Jessica M Rawson, "The Reuse of Ancient Jades", *Chinese Jades* - Colloquies on Art and Archaeology in Asia no 18, London: SOAS 1997, pp.171-188

Rawson 1998a
Jessica M Rawson, "Commanding the Spirits. Control Through Bronze and Jade", *Orientations* 1998.2, pp.33-45

Rawson 1998b
Jessica M Rawson, "Transformed into Jade: Changes in Material in the Warring States, Qin and Han Periods", *East Asian Jade: Symbol of Excellence*, HK: The Chinese University of Hong Kong, 1998, vol 2, pp.125-136

Rawson 2007
Jessica M Rawson, "The First Emperor's tomb – The afterlife universe", *The First Emperor China's Terracotta Army* (ed Jane Portal), London: The British Museum Press, 2007, pp.114-145

Rawson 2012
Jessica M Rawson, "The Han Empire and its Northern Neighbours: The Fascination of the Exotic", *The Search for Immortality - Tomb Treasures of Han China* (ed James CS Lin), New Haven: Yale University Press, 2012, pp.23-36

Seidel 1987
Anna Seidel, "'Traces of Han Religion in Funerary Texts Found in Tombs" in *Dokyo to shokyo bunka* (ed Akizuki Kan'ei), Tokyo: Hirakawa, 1987, pp.678-714

Selbitschka 2013
Armin Selbitschka, "The tomb complex and its hidden secrets", *Qin: The Eternal Emperor and His Terracotta Warriors* (ed Maria Khayutina), Zurcher: Bernisches Historisches Museum, 2013, pp.144-154

Shaughnessy 1999
Edward L Shaughnessy, "Western Zhou History", *The Cambridge History of Ancient China—from the Origins of Civilization to 221 BC* (ed Loewe and Shaughnessy), Cambridge: Cambridge University Press, 1999, pp.292-351

Shaughnessy 2013
Edward L Shaughnessy, "The Zhou Dynasty and the Birth of the Son of Heaven", *Qin: The Eternal Emperor and His Terracotta Warriors* (ed Maria Khayutina), Zurcher: Bernisches Historisches Museum, 2013, pp.17-25

Shelach 2014
Gideon Shelach, "Collapse or transformation? Anthropological and archaeological perspectives on the fall of Qin", *Birth of An Empire: The state of Qin revisited* (ed by Yuri Pines, Lothar von Falkenhausen, Gideon Shelach, and Robin Yates), London: University of California Press, 2014, pp.113-138

Sun 2017
Zhixin Jason Sun (ed), *Age of Empires - Art of the Qin and Han Dynasties*, New York: The Metropolitan Museum of Art, 2017

Thorp 1980
Robert L Thorp, "Burial Practices of Bronze Age China", *The Great Bronze Age of China*, New York: The Metropolitan Museum, 1980, pp.51-66

Thorp 1981-2
Robert L Thorp, "The Sui Xian Tomb: Re-Thinking the Fifth Century", *Artibus Asiae* 43 (1981-82), pp.67-110

Thorp 1987
Robert L Thorp, "Mountain Tombs and Jade Burial Suits: Preparing for Eternity in the Western Han", *Ancient Mortuary Traditions of China paper on Chinese Ceramic Funerary Sculptures*, 1987, pp.26-39

Thote 2013
Alain Thote, "Tombs of the Principality of Qin: Elites and Commoners", *Qin: The Eternal Emperor and His Terracotta Warriors* (ed Maria Khayutina), Zurcher: Bernisches Historisches Museum, 2013, pp.37-45

Wang 2007
Helen Wang, "Coins", *The First Emperor China's Terracotta Army* (ed Jane Portal), London: The British Museum Press, 2007, pp.80-82

Watson 1961
Burton Watson. *Records of the Grand Historian: Han Dynasty II*, New York and London: Columbia University Press, 1961

Watson 1993
Burton Watson, *Records of the Grand Historian: Qin*, Hong Kong and New York, Columbia University Press, 1993

Wu 1981
Wu Rongzeng吳榮曾. "Zhen mu wen zhong suo jian dao de Dong Han Dao wu guanxi鎮墓文中所見到的東漢道巫關係", *Wenwu* 1981.3, pp.56-63

Wu 1997
Wu Hung 巫鴻"The Prince of Jade Revisited", *Chinese Jades* - Colloquies on Art and Archaeology in Asia no 18, London: SOAS 1997, pp.147-170

Wu 1999
Wu Hung, "Art and Architecture of the Warring States Period", *The Cambridge History of Ancient Chin - from the Origins of Civilization to 221 BC* (ed Loewe and Shaughnessy), Cambridge: Cambridge University Press, 1999, pp.651-744

Xi'an 2006
*Xi'an Beijiao Qin mu*西安北郊秦墓, Xi'an: Shanqin chubanshe, 2006

Xu et al. 2008
Zhi Xu, Fan Zhang, Bosong Xu, Jingze Tan, Shilin Li, Chunxiang Li, Hui Zhou, Hong Zhu, Jun Zhang, Qingbo Duan, and Li Jin, "Mitochondrial DNA Evidence for a Diversified Origin of Workers Building Mausoleum for First Emperor of China", *Plos One*, 2008 October, vol 3, pp.1-7

Yates 2007
Robin Yates, "The rise of Qin and the military conquest of the Warring States", *The First Emperor – China's Terracotta Army* (ed Jane Portal), London: The British Museum Press, 2007, pp.31-35

Yü 1987
Yü Ying-Shih余英時 "O Soul, Come Back! A Study in the Changing Conceptions of the Soul and Afterlife in Pre-Buddhist China", *Harvard Journal of Asiatic Studies*, vol 47, no 2, December 1987, pp.363-395

Yuan 1990
Yuan Zhongyi袁仲一, *Qin Shihuangling bingmayong yanjiu* 秦始皇陵兵馬俑研究, Beijing: Wenwu chubanshe, 1990

Yuan 2002
Yuan Zhongyi 袁仲一, *Qinshihuangling de kaogu faxian yu yanjiu* 秦始皇陵的發現與研究, Xian: shaanxi renmin chubanshe, 2002

Yuan 2014
Yuan Zhongyi袁仲一, *Qin bingmayong de kaogu faxian yu yanjiu* 秦兵馬俑的發現與研究, Beijing: Wenwu chubanshe, 2014

Yuan and Liu 2009
Yuan Zhongyi and Liu Yu 袁仲一和刘钰, *Qin taowen xinbian*秦陶文新编, Beijing: wenwu chubanshe, 2009

Yuan et al. 2005
Yuan Bingqiang, Liu Shiyi, Yu Guoming, and Yang Mingsheng袁炳強, 劉士毅, 于國明,和楊明生, "Gravity and Magnetic Field Feature for Archaeology in Site of the Emperor Qinshihuang Mausoleum, China秦始皇帝陵遗址考古重磁力場特徵", *Earth Science*地球科學, 2005, vol 10, pp.1616-1620

Zhang et al 2006
Zhang Zaiming, Zhang Yongcao, Wang Qian, He Yiping, and Wang Ruifeng張在明, 張永超, 王謙, 何一平, 和王銳鋒, "xunyixian Qin zhidao yizhi kaocha baogao旬邑縣秦直道遺址考察報告", *Wenbo*, 2006, vol 3, pp.75-78

Zhang 2013
Zhang Zhanmin張占民, "Qin Shi Huang lingyuan jiguping yizhi秦始皇陵園擊鼓坪遺址秦始皇陵園擊鼓坪遺址", *Kaoguyuwenwu* 2013, vol 2, p.112

Zhang and Cao 2014
Zhang Weixing and Cao Wei張衛星和曹瑋, "Qinshihuangdi lingyuan neicheng beibu daolu yicun kantan jianbao 秦始皇帝陵园内城北部道路遗存勘探简报", *Qinshihuangdi ling bowuyuan yuankan* 秦始皇帝陵博物院院刊, 2014, vol 4, pp.6-9

Zhao 2008
Zhao Huacheng趙化成, "Qinshihuangling wenguanyong xingzhi jiexi秦始皇陵文官俑性質解析", *Wenwubao*文物報, 11th July 2008

ILLUSTRATION
ACKNOWLEDGEMENTS

Our thanks go to the respective copyright holders for granting permission to reproduce their images in this catalogue. Every attempt has been made to accurately trace copyright ownership. Should any errors have occurred they will be corrected in subsequent editions provided notification is sent to National Museums Liverpool.

Figs 1-3, 57-59, 70, 79, 83, 129 & inside back cover - Emperor Qin Shihuang's Mausoleum Site Museum

Fig 4 - © Peter Hermes Furian/123RF

Fig 5 - © feiyuwzhangjie/123RF

Figs 6, 11, 15, 31, 36 & 66 - Copied from original maps, © The Trustees of the British Museum

Fig 7 - © Culture Relics Press

Fig 8 - © Freer Gallery of Art and Arthur M Sackler Gallery, Smithsonian Institution, Washington, DC. Gift of Charles Lang Freer, F1916.118.

Fig 9 - © Freer Gallery of Art and Arthur M Sackler Gallery, Smithsonian Institution, Washington, DC. Acquired under the guidance of the Carl Whiting Bishop expedition, F1985.35.

Figs 10, 12 & 109 - © Fitzwilliam Museum, Cambridge

Figs 13, 14, 17-27, 30, 39-50, 54-56, 61, 64, 65, 68, 69, 71-78, 80-82, 84-90, 92, 97-107, 112-116, 119, 120, 124, 125, front cover & frontispiece - © Mr Ziyu Qiu

Fig 16 - © chiyu/123RF

Fig 28 - © Mercket75/flickr

Fig 29 - © Fiona Philpott

Fig 32 - Photograph © 2018 Museum of Fine Arts, Boston

Figs 33, 62, 63, 94-96, 110 & 117 - © National Museums Liverpool

Figs 34 & 127 - © Xianyang Museum

Fig 35 - © Snark/Art Resource, NY

Fig 37 - © Lu Bo'an/Xinhua/Alamy Live News

Fig 38 - © Liudmila Semenova/123RF

Fig 51 - © Bibliotheque Nationale, Paris, France/ Archives Charmet/Bridgeman Images

Figs 52, 126 & 128 - Metropolitan Museum of Modern Art, New York

Fig 53 - © bpk/Staatliche Kunstsammlungen Dresden/Herbert Boswank

Fig 60 - © Emperor Qin Shihuang's Mausoleum Site Museum

Fig 67 & inside front cover - © Adrian Wojcik/123RF

Fig 91, pp.2-3 & back cover - © Pongpipat Sriwaralak/123RF

Fig 93 - © British Library, London, UK/Bridgeman Images

Fig 108 - © Eddie Gerald/Alamy Stock Photo

Fig 111 - © Museum of the Nanyue King of the Western Han Dynasty

Figs 118 & 122 - © Zhongyi Yan

Fig 121 - © Nanjing Museum

Fig 123 - © Archaeological Site Museum of Nanyue Palace

鸣谢单位名称及人员姓名

	单位名称	人员姓名
主办单位	陕西省文物局 Shannxi Provincial Culture relics bureau	赵荣Zhao Rong、罗文利Luo Wenli、张彤Zhang Tong、刘拥政Liu Yongzheng、周亚群Zhou Yaqun、张晓英Zhang xiaoying、张阳Zhang Yang、刘嘉Liu jia
承办单位	陕西省文物交流中心 Shaanxi Cultural Heritage Promotion Center	文军 Wen Jun、吴海云Wu Haiyun、张正Zhang Zheng、高煜翔Gao Yuxiang、吕梦琪Lu Mengqi、孙强Sun Qiang
协办单位	秦始皇帝陵博物院 Emperor Qin's Mausoleum Site Museum	候宁彬Hou Ningbin、贾强Jia Qiang、周铁Zhou Tie、马生涛Ma Shengtao、郑宁Zheng Ning、夏寅Xia Yin、邵文斌Shao Wengbin、刘珺 Liu Jun、
参展单位	陕西历史博物馆 Shaanxi History Museum	强跃Qiang Yue、庞雅妮Pang Yani、梁彦民Liang Yanmin、贺达昕He Daxin、胡薇 Hu Wei、王西梅Wang Ximei、董理Dong Li、姜涛Jiang Tao、刘芃Liu Peng
	陕西省考古研究院 Shaanxi Archaeological Institute	李刚Li Gang、王小蒙Wang Xiaomeng、李恭Li Gong、秦造垣Qin Zaoyuan、刘思哲Liu Sizhe、赵艺蓬Zhao Yipeng、李坤Li Kun
	汉景帝阳陵博物院 Han Yang Ling Museum	李举纲Li Jugang、毕胜Bi Sheng、闫华军Yan Huajun、陈波Chen Bo、张琳Zhang Lin、石宁 Shi Ning
	咸阳博物馆 Xian Yang Museum	王晓谋Wang Xiaomou、严志敏Yan Zhimin、王亚庆Wang Yaqing、边永峰Bian Yongfeng
	咸阳市文物保护中心 Xian Yang Cultural Heritage Conservation Center	葛洪Ge Hong、陈秋歌、史泪力Shi Guli、许玲Xu Ling
	兴平市博物馆 Xing Ping Museum	马得翼Ma Deyi、蒙桃叶Meng Taoye
	长武县博物馆 Chang Wu County Museum	雷敏 LeiMing、曹红Cao Hong
	茂陵博物馆 Mao Ling Museum	王志杰 Wang Zhijie、魏乾涛Wei Qiantao、王敏霞Wang mixia
	宝鸡市考古工作队 Baoji Archaeological Working Team	刘军社Liu Junshe、辛怡华XingYihua、王颢Wang Hao、胡望林Hu Wanglin、张程Zhang Cheng
	陇县博物馆 Long Xian County Museum	王全军Wang Quanjun、孙晓利Sun Xiaoli、张智明Zhang Zhiming、
	岐山县博物馆 Qi Shan County Museum	徐永卫Xu Yongwei、白晶Bai Jing、张朝晖Zhang Zhaohui

INDEX

This index is in alphabetical, word-by-word order. It does not cover the contents list, foreword, notes, bibliography or illustrations list. Location references are to (1) page number and (2) page/figure number, e.g.

books, burning of, 50, 51 Fig.35
indicates that information concerning the burning of books by the First Emperor can be found on page 50, with an image on page 51.

Abbreviations: Fig = Figure

CHINA'S FIRST EMPEROR AND THE TERRACOTTA WARRIORS

TERRACOTTA WARRIOR PARTNERSHIPS

We would like to thank all the sponsors and donors
who have so generously supported this exhibition

SUPPORTED BY

First direct flight UK to Xi'an launches in 2018

KEYNOTE PARTNER

UK's number 1 China travel and tour specialist

MAJOR PARTNERS

FOYLE FOUNDATION   Unilever   SWIRE CHARITABLE TRUST

TERRACOTTA WARRIOR PARTNERS

SIGNATURE LIVING   QUILTER CHEVIOT INVESTMENT MANAGEMENT   London Stock Exchange Group

Sir David Henshaw   Andrew and Kelly Roscoe   Ian Rosenblatt OBE